ANXIETY, TRUST, and GRATITUDE

·

TRANSFORMATIVE WISDOM SERIES

THE TRANSFORMATIVE WISDOM SERIES engages the themes of spiritual, personal, and societal transformation, bringing to bear the timeless wisdom of the Eastern Orthodox Church and the cumulative wisdom of contemporary Western psychotherapies.

Vol. I: *Illumining Shame, Anger, and Forgiveness*
Vol. 2: *Anxiety, Trust, and Gratitude*
Vol. 3: *Loneliness or Fruitful Longing*
Vol. 4: *Race, Identity, and Reconciliation*

Also by the author:

Traditions of the Healing Church: Exploring the Orthodox Faith

ANXIETY, TRUST and GRATITUDE

Nun Katherine Weston, MA, LMHC
Foreword by Abbot Tryphon

WESTON COUNSELING, LLC
PUBLICATIONS
Indianapolis, Indiana
2020

Printed with the blessing of His Grace
✠ Longin
Serbian Orthodox Bishop of the Diocese
of New Gracanica and Midwestern America

Copyright © 2020 by Nun Katherine Weston

Weston Counseling, LLC
PO Box 88442
Indianapolis, IN 46208-0442

mk@westoncounseling.org

Cover photo: "An Autumn Evening in the Sax-Zim Bog," in Minnesota, by Popadija Xenia Franck. Used by permission.

About the Weston Counseling, LLC, logo: The nautilus shell presents a pattern of growth that God has used from the smallest sea creatures to the greatest cosmic nebulae. It is a metaphor for psychological healing: We cycle through themes, but at a greater breadth of healing each time. The Cross is our spiritual healing. At the center of both is a pearl— Christ Himself.

Weston Counseling, LLC, Publications
ISBN-13: 978-0-9983906-5-9

BISAC: REL012110
Religion / Christian Life / Spiritual Warfare

CONTENTS

Foreword

A Christian should never and for no reason worry,
for God's Providence carries him in its arms.
Our only care should be that we would
ever remain faithful to the Lord.[1]
— St Ignatius Brianchaninov

OURS IS DEFINITELY an age of anxiety, bottled up irritation, fears and unease, both ready to explode at any moment and running beneath the surface of people's actions and thoughts much of the time. This has proved to be all the more true in the light of recent events. And yet when we open the pages of the New Testament or read the divinely inspired teachings of the saints, we see them emphasizing how important it is not to worry and not to be fearful. Bridging the gap between what we are counseled to do and where we find ourselves at the moment can sometimes seem like a gulf impossible to cross.

Part of the reason for this unease is simply a greater flooding of noise in our lives—noise both within and without. Today's technological advancements have introduced noise into our lives in ways unthinkable to the ancients. Not more than a hundred years ago, most families found silence as an everyday experience, for when the sun went down, families nestled into warm corners of their parlors, and their kitchens, often reading books, or simply watching a crackling fire. Along with this quieting down of the day, silence was part of every evening.

Orthodox families were especially cognizant of the need to spend quiet time on the eve of the Sunday Liturgy, as well as great feasts of the Church, knowing that this silence served as a preparation time for receiving Christ's Body and Blood, during the celebration of the upcoming Liturgy. Silence was the means by which people accessed and deepened their relationship with God, and developed self-knowledge. Silence allowed them to live more harmoniously in our world, and actually listen for the voice of God speaking to their hearts. And this call to inner silence was not only some "special calling" for monks or clergy—it was for all Christians. It was for all who strove to live according to Christ's commandments.

Another common reason for the loss of inner peace in these times especially is a quickness to take offense at others' words and actions. The Christian who lives his life with internal strife and worry edifies neither other Christians, nor does he reflect anything of Christianity that would be attractive to those who have no faith. Such a person can even be a serious stumbling block for others, because his "religiosity" seems to many to be the cause of his weakness.

Saint Paul said that, *Love is not irritable or resentful … Love bears all things, hopes all things, endures all things* (I Cor. 13). If we are always complaining, weeping, or worrying, we are not living according to the directive of the Apostle Paul. Ungodly, spiritually unhealthy worry is very often based on a sentimentality of our Christian faith, which can create an atrophied, degenerated version of Orthodoxy that inspires no one, and ultimately leads to the death of our own soul.

The true Christian is to be patient with others, just as they themselves are in need of the patience of their friends and family. As Christians we are called to be a faithful people, yet we often act in a way as to betray ourselves as faithless. We ought to live by the power of God, yet we give in to a weakness that is subject to anxiety and fear. We are the children of the Most High, empowered by our God for a life of holiness and faith. Let us live with courage and faith, that we might acquire peace of heart and shine before all men the Light of Christ.

In the light of all of these common causes and manifestations of disquiet, unease, fear and anxiety, which ultimately have their root in the heart and soul of every human being, it is a blessing to have a short and straightforward work such as the book you are holding in your hands, which links where many find themselves today with the beginning steps necessary and helpful to better acquire that inner peace the Scriptures speak of that "passes all understanding" (cf. Php. 4:7).

May we all dedicate (and re-dedicate!) ourselves to the journey we are called to in the acquiring of this inner peace, and not only shine with the light of the Gospel upon our family and friends, but also to all those whom we encounter. We are all called to be God's vehicles for the light of His grace to shine in the world. May we all take heart and set out afresh on this difficult yet rewarding life's journey into the heart of God.

July 28, 2020
Holy Equal-to-the-Apostles Great Prince Vladimir
Enlightener of Russia

Abbot Tryphon
Igumen of the All-Merciful Saviour Monastery
Vashon Island, Washington

NOTES

[1] Rees, (Nun) Cornelia (Trans.). (2015). From a collection of spiritual sayings by *Foma*. Retrieved on July 29, 2020 from https://orthochristian.com/79283.html and the original Russian from https://foma.ru/svyatitel-ignatij-bryanchaninov-aforizmyi.html.

PREFACE

THE SOUL IS ONE. God's wisdom, freely shared with our human race, is one. We use, however, the prism of our minds so as to differentiate that ray of wisdom into the many and various disciplines of human endeavor. So I, too, have used that prism to distinguish the lights of spiritual and psychological contemplation. But the soul that we contemplate is one.

You have in your hands the capstone of an eighteen-year project of contemplating the spiritual and psychological aspects of human life. During that time I have journeyed with you, my readers, through a range of human experiences and emotions that bring us both joy and sorrow: Loneliness, shame, anger, and forgiveness. Slavery, trauma, and freedom. We have journeyed to these places together, and now we complete that journey with *Anxiety, Trust, and Gratitude*.

I did once attempt an essay to answer the question of God's presence when innocents endure trauma. I developed it to the highest reach of my understanding at the outset of my counseling education. But experience as a therapist showed me that "Where was God?" or "What is the meaning of my suffering?" was the first question asked and the last answer revealed to those who have lived through trauma. So I can only offer my encouraging ear to those who tell me of these passages of life. At this point I would fear preempting another's triumphant moment of discovering the pearl of meaning buried in the battlefield of life. Hence I lay down my pen.

The first essay, "Anxiety and Trust in Times of Turmoil," was presented in 2011 at the annual Fellowship of St. Moses the Black Conference in Livonia, Michigan. This was well into the Great Recession. The theme has only increased in timeliness in our current experience of the pandemic's restructuring of our lives and livelihoods, as well as the racial upheavals of 2020. Since the essay is rooted in the Bible and in universal human experiences, I did not feel that it needed updating, but was rather eager to finally make it accessible, hoping that it will give some readers an anchor of sorts.

A version of "Anxiety and Trust in Attachment" was presented in 2009 to the Fellowship conference in Indianapolis. It served as the foundation of an expanded presentation the following year for the International Orthodox Psychotherapy Conference in Chicago. The longer version has tables of the Hebrew Bible and Greek New Testament vocabulary for the many and varied experiences of love and connection. And it goes more deeply into the psychology of the attachment of infants to their parents. It was translated into Greek for the periodical *Psychēs Dromois (The Ways of the Soul)*, published November, 2014, volume 8. I would love to publish the original English, but maybe another day. It was written for a professional audience and I don't want to slow the reading tempo of this volume by including it in its entirety here.

A preliminary reading of "Gratitude: The Fruit of Trust" was presented in Columbia, South Carolina in 2018. My months-long meditation on gratitude was helpful to my own spiritual life and also carried into my work with clients. Gratitude is so very simple; yet for us Westerners it can be so very difficult. Taking our blessings for granted is the more comfortable choice, although we rarely notice how spiritually isolating that is. If nothing else, I hope this volume will serve as a reminder to practice this virtue more intentionally.

My heartfelt appreciation goes to Abbot Tryphon for the foreword. In it he speaks a word of peace for our hearts from the solitude and peace of his hermitage on Vashon Island. We first met in the 1980s at the outset of my Orthodox journey and I rejoice to have our paths cross again.

I again express my gratitude to Monk Cosmas (Shartz), writer and translator, who kindly made editorial comments on the second essay on attachment—as well as several essays in the other volumes of this series. My appreciation again goes to editorial readers Hieromonk Alexii (Altschul) who is my monastery's spiritual father, Popadija Xenia Franck, née Lundeen, and Theodosia Boyd. Without the help of my patient monastic sisters at St. Xenia's in Indianapolis, my books would never see the light of day. Thank you again to Popadija Xenia for the peaceful cover photograph and layout advice.

As always, my heartfelt appreciation goes to the Fellowship of St. Moses the Black and all affiliated with it for drawing these reflections out of me. And now, as of Juneteenth[1] of this year, for entrusting me to be its president. The Fellowship is here "to equip Orthodox Christians for the ministry of racial reconciliation and to share the Orthodox Christian faith with African Americans and people of color."

July 25, 2020
Feast of the Trojerucitsa icon of the Mother of God

Nun Katherine Weston

---

[1] Juneteenth: a holiday celebrating the emancipation of enslaved people in the U.S. Lincoln's Emancipation Proclamation was signed in January of 1863. However, it was not until Union troops reached Texas that the enslaved people in the farthest reaches of the Confederacy learned of their free status on June 19, 1865.

First Essay, 2011:
Anxiety and Trust
in Times of Turmoil ·

Watch over yourselves,
lest your hearts be weighed down
with overindulgence and drunkenness,
and cares of this life (Lk. 21:34a).

A NXIETY IS NOTHING NEW—not even the intensity with which we experience it today in a time of political and financial uncertainty. In the Bible it all begins with Cain who, after slaying his brother, Abel, suffers from terrible anxiety. The Lord pronounced this sentence on him: *thou shalt be groaning and trembling upon the earth* (LXX, Gen. 4:12). So as to appreciate the rich lessons of the Scriptures, we will lay a foundation of the biblical language used for the experiences of anxiety and trust. We will seek insight for both the cause of the problem and its cure from the Bible, Orthodox writers—especially that great light from Africa, St. Macarios the Great—and from modern psychology. Ultimately we hope to articulate how the Lord Jesus Christ offers us true and lasting peace. The goal of this exploration is to enhance our vision of how Orthodoxy offers solutions for modern problems—in this case, for anxiety in a time of crisis. With that let us begin with the Bible.

1

The Authorized Version

NOW LET'S TAKE A BRIEF LOOK at anxiety words in the Authorized (King James) Version of the Bible and in the original languages. This makes it possible to identify important passages on anxiety and also to find the commentaries by St. Macarios who left us homilies on scriptural passages.

The King James was published in 1611. I note this because the English language has always been a work in progress and the words that denote anxiety have been changing over time. Four hundred years ago when the King James was in the making, "care" both meant "anxiety" and meant "concern" in a positive sense. But since the words "anxiety," "preoccupation," and "stress" assumed their modern meanings, "care" is often now used in the context of caregiving, or even as a synonym for "love" (see Harper, 2010). The Authorized Version, however, uses "care" to mean "anxiety." We will look briefly at the original languages and then get back to this point.

Biblical Hebrew and Greek

NOT SURPRISINGLY, the Bible has several ways of expressing the experience of anxiety. Hebrew has a number of words that literally mean to tremble or shake, and which figuratively describe strong emotion. The Old Testament describes anxiety in terms of observable behavior; this is perhaps the most powerful way to describe emotions because their bodily signs are part of our human nature, often transcending time and culture.

In addition, both the Old and New Testaments use specific anxiety vocabulary. Some words convey the sense of anxious waiting or being troubled in mind. Other very important words convey the ideas of worry, preoccupation, and negative expectations. If we want to search the King James for key scriptures, these three are all translated as "care." Thus "care" comes down to us as the most important anxiety word in the English language Bible.

The Bible teachings have a strong focus on *care* as being preoccupied or distracted with worldly concerns. This is seen as a strong impediment to following Jesus Christ. Learning to avoid distraction is just as important as learning to trust in God and so avoid worry. We will develop these themes as the essay progresses. Now back to the story of Cain.

Anxiety in the Scriptures

"GROANING AND TREMBLING and tossed *shalt thou be upon the earth"*—this is St. Macarios's rendering of the divine sentence. He then universalizes the meaning, saying that while this groaning and trembling was outwardly manifest in Cain, it is the inner experience, or likeness, of every fallen human soul.

> After falling from the commandment and entering the sinful state, the race of Adam has acquired that likeness in secret; it is tossed about with shifting thoughts *[logismoi]* of fear and terror and every kind of commotion [Mason, 1921, p. 39].

The beginning of anxiety is the general sinful human state that causes us to inwardly groan and tremble. In the Hebrew Bible, very concrete terms are used to indicate inner realities. The groaning and trembling, and being "tossed about with shifting thoughts of fear and terror" are our common fate. This anxiety is part of what Jesus Christ came to heal because it so torments us.

Let us now look at the prophetic words of the Lord Jesus about a very anxious time for His earthly followers. He spoke to Peter, as the eleven accompanied Him on that final walk to Gethsemane: *Simon, Simon, behold, Satan hath desired to have you, that he may sift you as wheat* (Lk. 22:31). We will begin by looking at that powerful sifting metaphor, for a metaphor is only as effective as the shared understanding of its physical and cultural basis. So much has changed since the time when Jesus spoke using common, everyday images from an agrarian culture, that the shared basis for biblical metaphor is eroding.

After a little cultural research, I offer you this translation of the Lord's words: *Simon, Simon, Satan has desired to winnow all of you as grains of wheat* (Lk. 22:31). The heap of grain in a winnow, or winnowing basket, is shaken vigorously by the winnower and tossed into the air with a wheeling motion. Jesus' use of this metaphor carries forward the Hebraic use of the idea of shaking to describe overwhelming emotions and experiences. As the Therapist[1] of souls He forewarned the Apostles so that they would not utterly despair as Judas actually did. The winnowing metaphor captures the turbulence and confusion the Apostles went through during that time. As their Leader was arrested and tried, each one of them experienced the arrest and trial of his beliefs about Jesus, their mission, their future, and their God. They were anxious and confused. They did not know whom to trust; they locked themselves in for safety in a world where the bottom had just dropped out from under them. If this anxiety is the fate of the Apostles themselves, how much more must we expect to share in it!

St. Macarios expanded on this metaphor. Speaking in a time when people understood the earth to be flat, he likened the whole earth, and all earthly affairs, to a winnowing basket. In this winnow he envisions, not the eleven Apostles, but all of humanity from the time of Adam's fall.

> The inhabitants of the earth, the children of this age, are like grain placed in the winnowing basket of this earth, winnowed by restless, impassioned thoughts [*logismoi*] of this world, and by the ever-surging waves of earthly affairs, by desires, and by tangled notions of materiality. In the winnow of earthly circumstance, Satan buffets and tosses the souls of the whole sinful race of man, ever since Adam fell by transgressing the command-

---

[1] The New Testament uses three verbs for Christ's healing work, *iaomai, sozo,* and *therapeuo.* Respectively "heal," "save," and "carefully attend to." It is in that last sense that I call Him Therapist.

ment, coming under the Commander of Evil. From the time he gained this authority, he does nothing but winnow with deceitful and agitated thoughts all the sons of this age, and dash them in the winnowing basket of the earth [St. Macarios the Great, Homily V, *PG* 65:496. Author's translation].

St. Macarios really condensed his insights in that passage; let us unpack it some. It seems to me there are different elements to the winnowing process: the external and the internal. Yet he is impressionistic in how he employs the metaphor so that we cannot get too caught up in looking for exact correspondences.

The external elements are life's circumstances and the "ever-surging waves of earthly affairs." The internal are first, our "impassioned thoughts of this world"; second, "desires"; and third, our "tangled notions of materiality." Impassioned thoughts are emotionally charged thoughts: thoughts of this world bound up with irrational desire, anxiety, or anger; born of our fleshly nature rather than our spiritual. Our desires, the second factor, are the source of both our anxiety and our anger. The prospect of losing or not attaining what we desire makes us anxious. The anxiety makes us angry at whatever we see as frustrating our fulfillment. The third factor, "tangled notions of materiality," refers to a deeply confused sense of meaning. We suffer from a basic failure to let the material order point us back to the hand of the Creator and so derive a correct understanding of our relationship to the physical realm. Finally, Satan himself gained the authority to dash us about in the "surging waves of earthly affairs," igniting impassioned thoughts and desires, and inhibiting any attempt at spiritual orientation. This is where the human race was after the first sin and where we still are today. The remedy that Scripture proposes is trust. This is a dominant theme of the whole of Scripture.

Godly Trust: The Remedy for Anxiety

Trust in the Scriptures

L ET US NOW TOUCH LIGHTLY on how "trust" is used in the Scriptures. In one sense, where people put their "trust," in the Hebrew Bible, is where they flee for refuge or take shelter, again a very concrete sense. For me it conjures up the image of running to a large rock to escape the danger of wild beasts or military enemies. From the point of view of our relationship with God, however, it is just the same as young children who run to their father or mother when they are frightened.

The other sense of the word "trust" is to endure patiently until the Lord rescues. This is seen in the Book of Job. Thus the Hebrew Bible gives us two meanings that combine beautifully to illustrate that we are both to flee to God for refuge and then to endure patiently until He rescues us.

When the Hebrew Scriptures were translated into the Greek Septuagint a few centuries before Christ, the Hebrew words for taking shelter were rendered in the Greek by two primary words, "to hope" and "to have confidence based on solid evidence." This is no blind trust, but a trust proven through the centuries in which the Hebrew people took shelter in the God of Israel and learned that He was indeed trustworthy, unlike the pagan gods. The Jewish people, at the time the Septuagint was translated, hailed it as a divinely inspired work. The new understanding of trust reflected, not just the language differences between the Hebrew and the *Koine* Greek but, I believe, also a maturation of the Hebrews' faith in God.

Today, in the region of the Midwest where I live, we are treated to billboards that caution travelers: "Avoid hell. Trust Jesus today." This pared-down theology assumes that by an act of mind and will, the reader can "sign up" for Jesus and then be issued a "spiritual security card." He can then whip out this card and gain sanctuary from the yawning gates of hell when the time comes. Now this is the antithesis of the trust we are speaking of here, the trust taught and illustrated in the Bible.

The Scriptures are so full of passages on trust or distrust in God, with the respective consequences of each, that it is hard to pick just a few. But having spoken of Cain earlier, let us begin by reexamining his case. The trouble all began when he and his brother, Abel, both agreed to offer sacrifice to God. Abel's was pleasing because he offered his best; Cain's was rejected because he did it offhandedly. Still, God did not reject Cain, but only rejected the sacrifice. God counseled Cain like a beloved son, Why are you sad and downcast? You were right to bring the sacrifice, but you sinned, did you not, when you failed to divide to me the right portion? (Cf. Gen. 4:6–7). Then to console him, the Lord makes the rather astonishing promise to place Abel under his authority and rule. Cain did not trust in God's solution and followed his own lights. He killed his brother and became subject to anxiety, as we explored above.

Abraham, on the other hand, was actually tested by God with the command to make sacrifice of his only son and heir (see Gen. 22:1–18). Even though it made no sense in human terms, he went and obeyed. This was not blind faith. This was confidence based on solid evidence. Had not God given him a son past all expectation in his old age? Based on his encounter with God in the miraculous birth of Isaac, Abraham trusted that God could revive his son and heir from the dead. He was able to fulfill the counsel, later given in the Book of Proverbs, *Trust in the Lord with all your heart and do not rely on your own understanding* (Pr. 3:5).

Two great commentators

METROPOLITAN ANTHONY BLOOM gives a wonderful discussion of this kind of faith and trust in his book, *God and Man*. He distinguishes between the childhood faith that we inherit from parents (or others who go before us), and the mature faith that comes after we have had a spiritual encounter with the unseen realm of God. In interpreting Hebrews 11 he says, "faith is defined as 'certainty of things unseen.' We usually lay the stress upon the 'things unseen' and forget the 'certainty' about them" (1971/2004, p. 45).

He also turns to St. Macarios the Great who clearly lived by trust in God. Here I quote Metropolitan Anthony, who first quotes and then interprets St. Macarios:

> "The experience of God, the vision of the world in God, is something which can happen only at a moment when all our thoughts, all emotions, are arrested to such a degree that we can no longer both be within the experience, perceive the things, and step out of the experience, watch ourselves and analyze what is going on. The moment when an experience is 'lived' is a moment when we cannot observe it." And he says that this would be quite sufficient for someone who has had an experience of God. He would not wish to go back to another stage. But he also says, "God has concern, not only for those who have this experience, but also for the people who haven't got it; that someone should come to them as a witness of things unseen, and yet experienced, real, and he steps back away from them." At that moment begins, he says, the realm of faith. The certitude remains even though the experience is already of the past; the certainty is there because what has happened to him is as certain as anything around him, is tangible, visible, perceived by the senses, so that the moment of faith begins as a result of a first contact with the invisible, discovered, disclosed, somehow [Bloom, 1971/2004, pp. 46–47].

Metropolitan Anthony goes on to assert that any trust in God that is not based on solid evidence is liable to crumble in times of turmoil. It crumbles, he says, because we see it as a failure, not of our *concepts* about God, but of *God Himself.* We see it, not as an opportunity to broaden our narrow understanding, but a failure of any possibility to make meaning of the unseen, or even as a failure of the unseen to ultimately exist. He counsels us to get a realistic picture of where we are on the road to real trust and act accordingly.

> We ask ourselves whether we have any experience of it. If we haven't, it must remain a field to be investigated. It remains a field that was conveyed to us by someone who knows, but which is not known to us. It is promising, but it must hold its promise for the future. We cannot yet say "I know for certain, I understand with experience" [1971/2004, pp. 47–48].

Impediments and Global Anxiety

Anxiety is nothing new. Not even anxiety about an increasingly unbalanced economy and global catastrophe. The earth itself is a winnow, constantly shaking and tossing the whole human race. Perhaps the question is not so much "whence comes our anxiety," but "whence come earthly thoughts of peace and security?" This shallow belief in earthly security that suppresses the appetite for God is a "pathological security."

On a societal level I see some trends that work together to foster the sense of "pathological security." One is an exaggerated pride in the American meritocracy system which has reached mythic proportions; rationalism and materialism are interrelated with this. Meritocracy is a system where people get ahead based on their personal merits, rather than on personal influence and connections. It allows people who are born into social and financial disadvantage to rise to the top. This certainly has happened to an important degree in our society, more than in some European countries today that function on a system of seniority. There, even talented young people with multiple advanced degrees fail to find work. In still other countries employment comes from personal connections. I have even heard of a case where a young man, who had lost his father, could not find work because it was the father's prerogative to make those connections. So I am not knocking meritocracy, not even in its uneven manifestations.

When I speak of the *myth* of meritocracy, I am pointing to this: "Self-made" success stories routinely fail to give credit to fortuitous timing, unique opportunities, and prosperity's other background themes (see Gladwell, 2008). Success stories told in this self-aggrandizing way—denuded of contextual elements—are held up to the rest of society as models for emulation. Depend on your own efforts! Develop your potential to the fullest! God has no place in the narrative.

While our rational Western culture teaches us to put all our trust in our own analytical powers, skill, and effort, our consumer culture teaches us to place our trust in our wealth and possessions. As long as these work for us, then there is a sense of security. When these fail and people are not schooled in trusting God in a radical way, then the resulting anxiety can be overwhelming and even lead some to take their lives. As the psalmist says: *Lo, this is the man that made not God his helper, but trusted in the abundance of his riches, and strengthened himself in his vanity* (LXX, Ps. 51:7). This is the face that anxiety wears in our time of economic turbulence.

I do not mean to imply that people who suffer anxiety in these times may not believe in God and even be devout church goers. Many of us *believe* in God but do not fully *depend* on God; we still depend on ourselves.

Psychological impediments

IN THE PSYCHOLOGICAL REALM, moreover, there are levels and depths of believing. There are core thoughts around which the personality forms and coalesces much as our flesh forms around our bones. Obviously there are also many beliefs on the level of the rational mind. The deep beliefs I'm speaking of, however, are out of conscious sight and control. It takes special work and insight to find and change them. It is on this level that a person trusts or does not trust in God, even while outwardly confessing Him. This deep level of trust is initially developed through early experience with childhood caregivers. It may be hard to run to God in times of trouble if we had difficult experiences running to our parents.

All people, even atheists, carry deep within them a sense of what God is like—whether He be benevolent, or aloof, or irrelevant, or persecutory. This is called a person's God image.[2] The God image lives on this deep level of unconscious thought from where it directs the religious and faith experience. A negative God image in a time of prosperity may not reveal itself. But it is in times of difficulty that people find out whether or not they really know how to trust in Someone apart from themselves. To place their cares in God's hands, remembering that *The rich have turned poor and gone hungry, but they that seek the Lord shall not be deprived of any good thing* (LXX, Ps. 33:10).

Sometimes exploring the extremes can help us be sensitive to the more subtle. So I will take an example from the adoption of children. Some children, when adopted after a rough experience with foster care, are unable to form a sustaining attachment with their new father and mother. They reach out to everyone or to no one while being unduly attached to their belongings. This is called Reactive Attachment Disorder. I know this may sound harsh or counterintuitive, but some adoptive families have found success by embracing an austere way of life. They remove from the children all the baggage they bring with them, giving them instead, just the necessities. Then the new parents can begin to coax the children into a healthy attachment relationship with themselves.

This entrance of the children into their adoptive family closely parallels the way prospective monks and nuns enter into the spiritual family or monastery. They embrace poverty in order that their affections will not be scattered among all

---

[2] See pp. 48–49 below for more background on the God image.

their possessions; then God can coax them into an intimate attachment relationship with Himself. In an age of extreme materialism, it seems to me that we all have a bit of Reactive Attachment Disorder with respect to God. Perhaps God is giving us the opportunity to shift our primary attachments from material prosperity to Him.

St. Paisios the New of Mount Athos speaks with deep conviction about the need to lead simpler lives if we would avoid escalating anxiety. He helped me see how self-reliance and materialism are interconnected: We pursue gadgets and appliances that allow us to do everything for ourselves and not be interdependent with one another as in a healthy Christian family or society. We become more and more frantic trying to earn enough to keep abreast of these artificial material needs, and we lose the peace and comfort that come from spending real time with loved ones (see St. Paisios, 2006). Even if we want to live more traditionally, society does not support us in that aim. Making life changes to reduce anxiety and live closer to God is a heroic undertaking.

How anxiety slips in — on the societal level

THE "PATHOLOGICAL SECURITY" discussed above does not really end up working for anyone. Anxiety slips through on many fronts. Not only is anxiety the lot of fallen humans in general, it is especially the lot of those who have built their success on the sufferings of others. Our entire Western culture, which increasingly objectifies everything and everyone, has built success on the sufferings of the natural realm, undeveloped nations, and the voiceless and invisible in society. To the degree that these victims are indignant, according to St. Paisios of Mount Athos, the successful suffer anxiety.

> [A]ll those who commit injustice and do not ask for forgiveness, end up haunted by their conscience and the indigna-

tion of those they have treated unjustly. For if the wronged do not forgive and [they] complain, then the unjust are tormented and suffer very much. They cannot sleep. They feel like they are at the mercy of crashing waves that twist them around from every side. It's a mystery how the perpetrator is informed of this!... [T]he victim's pain tears the unjust into pieces! It does not matter where he may be, in Australia or in Johannesburg; as long as the person he has treated unfairly is indignant with him, he cannot find peace [St. Paisios, 2006, p. 88].

Do we defraud tribal peoples for affordable petroleum? Then we defraud ourselves of peace. Do we import foods from Central America in such a way that the farmers go hungry? Then we will hunger for tranquility. Do we import goods and clothing made by unregulated child labor or in sweatshops or prisons? Then we purchase anxiety with them. Do we increase national debt for our own comfort leaving our children and grandchildren enslaved by this debt? Lord have mercy.

Yet these are not personal choices for the great majority of us. The economic and supply chains are only partly visible; choices for society are made in closed board rooms. We would much rather that these injustices were not so, and yet they are. Reflecting on the intertwined nature of societal and personal evil, I. M. Andreev[3] said: "All for one and one for all are guilty: This is the essence of the social ethic of Christianity." We ourselves commit evils; through our sins [among which are malice and the condemnation of others] we "contribute our evil to the universal 'store-house of evil'" (1982, p. 39). Here is cause

---

[3] Ivan Michailovich Andreev (1894-1976) was a member of the Russian intelligentsia who converted back to the traditional Russian Orthodox Faith. He emigrated to the U.S. in 1950 and was a professor at Holy Trinity Orthodox Seminary, Jordanville, NY from 1950-1971. He was a prolific Russian-language author. His *Russia's Catacomb Saints* was translated into English by Fr. Seraphim Rose and published by the St. Herman of Alaska Brotherhood (1982).

for the godly sorrow that leads to repentance (cf. II Cor. 7:10) because even the most devout people in this land are inextricably bound up with unjust deeds, and even give leeway for them to happen. This is caused, not so much through outward things such as political outcomes, but through our own spiritual shortcomings. Andreev, however, goes on to say

> Weep, brothers and sisters! Do not be ashamed of these tears! ... Let your tears also be a fount of a different energy, an energy of good that fights against the energy of evil. ... Do not be ashamed to weep with tears of grief, compassion, and *repentance* [1982, p. 40].

Do we lack political power? Never mind. *For our conflict is not against blood and flesh, but against rulers, against authorities, against cosmic powers in this darkness, and against evil spiritual forces in the heavenly realm* (Eph. 6:12). We must protest in prayer, first of all through repentance, against the fallen tendencies in our own hearts.

Fortunately for us, we are far from alone in the battle against evil in our land. Interceding with us we have all the saints of America, those officially canonized and those known to God. We also have the enslaved martyrs of America who paid in blood for their faith in Christ just as much as the martyrs of the first centuries.[4] Let our prayers soar aloft on two wings of spiritual power—repentance and the intercession of the saints—to fight injustice from the inside out. And so, perhaps, we may be awarded a compassionate, non-complacent peace—the peace that comes when we cease defending our hearts against the pain of others.

---

[4] See *An Unbroken Circle:* Chap. 7, "The Legacy of a Suffering Church: The Holiness of American Slaves" by Prof. Albert Raboteau and Chap. 8, "The Call of the Righteous Slave Confessors" by Fr. Damascene Christensen. See also *Wade in the River: The Story of the African Christian Faith* by Fr. Paisius Altschul (now Hieromonk Alexii).

How anxiety slips in — on the personal level

THERE IS ANOTHER WAY that anxiety slips in, despite our best efforts to sidestep it. It seems to be transmitted from generation to generation in families. In an ideal setting, the parents would have a deep level of trust in God so that the children grow up in a worry-free environment. What often happens is just the opposite: Parents who are good Westerners put their trust in their own abilities and possessions and, as a result, have plenty of worries. Little children are by nature emotional sponges; they relieve their parents by carrying some of these burdensome feelings for them. This can come to seem so normal to the children that when they mature, this anxiety is their emotional "home base." It may seem so normal that when the Church speaks of "laying aside all earthly care," that notion may seem irresponsible or may go across the dictates of what feels like conscience. In family therapy we use the term "family rules" for these dictates.

Another important way that anxiety slips in is through our Western rationalism. If the news outlet, for example, gives financial or employment statistics, those become the hard facts we are up against. On the spiritual level our minds are far more than mere objective observers of "facts." Our beliefs about reality function as prayers, bringing about their own fulfillment. In other words, if there are five jobs and a hundred rationalists applying for them, then five will get the jobs and ninety-five will not. On the other hand, if there are five jobs and a hundred prayerful people applying for them, I believe that God would multiply the work as He multiplied the loaves and fishes. Physics has shown that observation can affect the phenomena being observed. Shouldn't we, as faithful Christians, be much more open to the idea that the way we see human affairs affects the outcome? A belief in limitation is just as much a prayer as a belief in God's abundance and generosity. Cold rationalism does not leave room for God and thus opens wide the door of our soul to the buffeting winds of anxiety.

Laying Aside All Care

Anxiety is the common lot of fallen human beings; yet the Lord, as the Therapist of souls, commands us to be without care. How is this possible? Let us look at the 21st chapter of Luke. The Lord instructs His followers on the signs that will precede His Second Coming and how to prepare: *Men's hearts,* He tells them, *will be failing them for fear, and for looking after those things which are coming on the earth: for the powers of heaven shall be shaken.... So likewise ye, when ye see these things come to pass, know ye that the kingdom of God is nigh at hand.... And take heed to yourselves, lest at any time your hearts be overcharged with surfeiting, and drunkenness, and cares of this life, and so that day come upon you unawares* (Lk. 21:26, 31 & 34).

I wish to focus on this last verse first. How does your experience of the passage change as we vary it with more modern word choices? *Watch yourselves so your hearts don't get weighed down with overindulgence and drunkenness, and the anxiety of daily life. ...with preoccupation with life's daily concerns. ... with the stress of everyday life.* In my experience, the newer words hit closer to home.

My next question is: Why did the Lord put "the stress of everyday life" on a par with "overindulgence and drunkenness?" This passage has layers of meaning. On one level, He uses this sequence of concerns to warn us against being swallowed up by the things that pass away, lest we be found wanting when we face eternity. In the context of our examination of anxiety and trust, this juxtaposition brings to mind our very human tendency to rely on overindulgence, sometimes in social gatherings, sometimes alone, as our way of relieving and temporarily forgetting our stress. Often this "remedy" will end up increasing the stress because overindulgence leads to accidents, careless words, and impulsive actions. So we should avoid getting caught up in a vicious cycle of stress and inebriation. This cycle makes the heart dull, putting us in danger of being spiritually asleep at the moment of the Lord's reckoning.

In fact, this passage is of such importance that it is quoted in the Cherubic Hymn sung during the Divine Liturgy. It says that we, who mystically represent the cherubim by singing to the Thrice-holy Trinity, should lay aside "all earthly cares." "All earthly cares" is how the phrase is usually rendered in the English. In the Greek the phrase means to lay aside "the fragmented concerns pertaining to daily life." The idea, again, is of being divided and scattered by many concerns. In English the phrase differs between the King James and the Divine Liturgy; in the Greek, the Cherubic Hymn quotes exactly the phrase from Luke 21, above, for "the anxiety of daily life," "the preoccupation with life's daily concerns," or "the stress of everyday life."

And why do we lay aside the stress and preoccupations of life during the Liturgy? So that "we may receive the King of All invisibly upborne by the angelic hosts." Literally this alludes to how the Roman emperors were carried aloft by their soldiers (see Gogol, 1985/2014, p. 45). Mystically, however, it recalls the Second Coming of Christ described in Luke 21, above.

So how do we take responsibility for our lives and still avoid the vicious cycle of stress and inebriation? This is where trust comes in. The daily needs of life were given us by God, after the banishment of our first parents from Paradise, as a way to live in constant dialogue with Him. That is, when living in Paradise free from all want and anxiety, the first parents forgot God. As a remedy, God gave bodily needs and daily concerns so that we would turn to Him again (see St. Symeon, 11th cent./1994). This requires enormous trust.

It requires trust in God, of course. It also involves trust in the healing process He has for us. It involves trust that if we stop turning questions over in our mind in order to spend time with God, we will not miss the inspired answer we've been searching for. It's easy enough to lay aside our concerns in the trance-like state that comes from sensory overindulgence—whether in food, drink, entertainment, or social networking. But to pray, we have to lay aside our anxieties in a state of spiritual sobriety. We can approach this by choosing to refocus on the worship service; we can equally approach this by choosing to pray about our daily-life concerns. Both approaches serve the same aim of bringing us closer to God and strengthening our trust in Him. God wishes us to live in a state of prayer and attentiveness to our inner state.

In a psychological approach people are sometimes taught to imagine a container large enough to store all their worries, to fill it and to lock it away somewhere. During the Divine Liturgy we "commend ourselves, one another, and all our lives unto Christ our God." That is, we recognize that God is in reality, not in imagination, spacious enough to hold us in His heart and our worries in His hand. The monastic Fathers talk about developing a radical sense of being alone with God. They say that to enter deeply into prayer we have to know that there is no one and nothing in the universe except oneself and God. We may need to try different approaches to reach that realization. As things come to mind in contradiction to this, we can commend them to God. When all these burdens float away, how light the soul feels! How it rejoices in God! If our parents used us as a "container" for their anxiety, how great it is to discover that God is a different kind of Parent. He wants us to contain His grace and blessings, not His "worries" or rather His concerns.

Simon, Simon, Satan has desired to winnow all of you as grains of wheat, but I have interceded for you, that your own faith may not fail. When you have come back, then strengthen your brothers (Lk. 22:31–32). The Lord, in His mercy, does not leave us helplessly to be winnowed by the anxieties and tragedies of life. He uses the winnowing basket of the earth to convince us, over time, of the futility of being attached to the earthly things that perish. He knows our measure and he uses the strong, the more experienced, to establish the weak, even as Simon Peter strengthened his brother apostles. He desires us to develop stability of mind and will through the incessant outward turmoil. St. Macarios the Great describes Christians not as people who look outwardly different from those in the world—for it is possible to look outwardly different and yet to share in the same worldly disposition—but as people who are inwardly different. Mature Christians are people who have arrived,

> through many conflicts and labors spread over a long time, at a fixed and settled condition of freedom from disturbance and of rest, no longer [winnowed] and wave-tossed by unquiet and vain thoughts [Mason, 1921, p. 40].

Conclusion

THE CURE GOD PROPOSES for our anxieties is a costly cure. It is not "cheap grace" as Dietrich Bonhoeffer famously expressed it (see Bonhoeffer, 1937/1995). It involves taking stock of ourselves: To what degree has self-sufficiency become an idol that we worship in place of the Living God? To what degree does our early life experience impede our ability to place trust outside of ourselves? To what degree is our heart dissipated by investment in caring for the things that perish? How can living more simply help us to be more carefree? Where can we simplify? How do we make heartfelt prayers for God's providence in the things that really matter? How can we learn to lay aside all earthly care so as to really develop a trusting attachment to God? How do we transfer our citizenship to heaven, as St. Macarios describes, and find ourselves among "…those which have been begotten from above, and have been translated in disposition and mind to another world, according as it is said, *But our citizenship is in heaven* (Php. 3:20)" (Mason, 1921, p. 40).

The cure involves taking the present turmoil as a blessing sent from the divine hand—a blessing and not a curse. The blessing is unveiled by our search for meaning. Anything that we can lose through national or even international turbulence, we will most certainly lose when we leave this world. Are we concerned for status? We will leave that behind. Are we concerned for comforts? We will leave those, too. Are we concerned for the basic necessities of life itself? Are we concerned for the needs of others? These latter are worthy things to pray for. Let us begin by seeking God and His reign first (see Mt. 6:33) and sinking all our cares in the abyss of His loving-kindness. He will add all these things to us.

ABBREVIATIONS

PG   Patrologiae Graecae. (1857-66) J.-P. Migne.

REFERENCES AND BIBLIOGRAPHY
FIRST ESSAY

American Psychiatric Association. (2000). *Diagnostic and statistical manual of mental disorders,* 4th ed., text revision. Washington, DC: American Psychiatric Association.

Andreev, Ivan M. (1982). *Russia's catacomb saints: Lives of the new martyrs,* (St. Herman of Alaska Brotherhood, Trans. & Ed.). Platina, CA: St. Herman of Alaska Brotherhood.

Altschul, (Priest) Paisius, (Ed.). (1997). *An unbroken circle: Linking ancient African Christianity to the African-American experience.* St. Louis, MO: The Brotherhood of St. Moses the Black.

_____. (2001). *Wade in the river: The story of the African Christian faith.* Kansas City, MO: CrossBearers.

Bloom, (Metropolitan) Anthony. (1971/2004). *God and man.* London: Darton, Longman & Todd, Ltd.

Bonhoeffer, Dietrich. (1937/1995). *The cost of discipleship.* (C. K. V. München & R. H. Fuller, Trans.). New York: A Touchstone Book, by Simon & Schuster.

Cozolino, Louis. (2006). *The neuroscience of human relationships: Attachment and the developing social brain.* New York: W. W. Norton & Co.

_____. (2010). *The neuroscience of psychotherapy: Healing the social brain,* 2nd ed. New York: W. W. Norton & Co.

Frankl, Viktor. (1959). *Man's search for meaning.* Boston: Beacon Press.

25

Gladwell, Malcolm. (2008). *Outliers: the story of success.* New York: Little, Brown and Company.

Gogol, Nikolai G. (1985/2014). *Meditations on the Divine Liturgy of the Holy Eastern Orthodox Catholic and Apostolic Church,* (Alexieff, L., Trans.), updated and revised 3rd ed. Jordanville, NY: Holy Trinity Monastery.

Harper, Douglas. (2010). *Online etymology dictionary.* www.etymonline.com. Retrieved July 17, 2010.

Macarios the Great, St. (4ᵗʰ cent./1903). Macarius the Egyptian: Spiritual Homilies. In the *Patrologiae Graecae,* vol. 34. Paris: J.-P. Migne.

Mason, Arthur J., (Trans.). (1921). *Fifty spiritual homilies of St. Macarius the Egyptian.* London: Society for Promoting Christian Knowledge, Macmillan. From http://openlibrary.org/books/ OL7250363M/ Fifty_spiritual_homilies_of_St._Macarius_the_Egyptian. Retrieved November 22, 2010.

Paisios the New, St. (C. A. Tsakiridou & M. Spanou, Trans.). (2006). *Spiritual Counsels,* Vol. I: *With pain and love for contemporary man.* Souroti, Thessaloniki: Holy Monastery "Evangelist John the Theologian."

Papadeas, (Protopresbyter) George L., (Compiler). (1971). *Greek Orthodox Holy Week and Easter Services.* Athens and New York: G. Tsiveriotis, Printer.

Schmidt, Shirley Jean. (2009). *The developmental needs meeting strategy: An ego state therapy for healing adults with childhood trauma and attachment wounds.* Gresham, OR: DNMS Institute, LLC.

Schwartz, Richard C. (1995). *Internal family systems therapy.* New York: Guilford.

Seraphim of Sarov, St., (Hieromonk S. Rose, Trans.). (19ᵗʰ cent./1996). *Little Russian philokalia, vol. I: Saint Seraphim of Sarov: spiritual instructions,* 4ᵗʰ ed. Platina, CA: St. Herman of Alaska Brotherhood.

Symeon the New Theologian, St. (Hieromonk S. Rose, Trans.). (11ᵗʰ cent./1994). *The first created man.* Platina, CA: St. Herman of Alaska Brotherhood.

Theophan the Recluse, St. (Revisor). (1978). *Unseen warfare: The spiritual combat and path to paradise of Lorenzo Scupoli.* Nicodemus of the Holy Mountain (Ed.), E. Kadloubovsky and G. E. H. Palmer (Trans.). Crestwood, N.Y.: St. Vladimir's Seminary Press.

•

Second Essay, 2009:
Anxiety and Trust
in Attachment

Early Church writers, especially the monks, recognized that we human beings have three basic capacities—the capacity to desire, the capacity to rise against, and the capacity to think. The things we desire are the things with which we develop attachment relationships. If anything hinders our access to the things we desire, we become angry. Thus, according to the traditional Orthodox writers, as we set out along the spiritual path, becoming conscious of our desires and attachments is the place to begin. We will never make progress in dealing with the sinful aspects of our anger if we do not heal our desiring nature and our attachments or relational bonds.

Attachment pertains to more than possessions; it concerns relationship, connectedness. Attachment means emotional investment—emotional energy invested somewhere as when we invest money in a bank, securities, or education. Attachment is the result of investing energy in God, other people, in behaviors, things, and substances. Here is a test: If we would experience turmoil on losing something then we are attached to it. As St. John of the Ladder says: "If anyone thinks he is without attachment to some object, but is grieved at its loss, then he is completely deceiving himself" (*Ladder* 2:11). It does not even have to be something we possess, it can even be our hopes and dreams.

Why, then, is attachment important? Not only does it mean relationship, connectedness; it means a pattern or style of relating—to a person, place, behavior, or object—that endures over time. In our lives the centrality of an attachment consists, not in how gratifying we find the relationship, but in the strength or energy of its bond. Attachment determines what we care about.

Scope and objective

IN THIS ESSAY we will look at attachment within human relationships, in our spiritual lives, and even within ourselves—our hearts and minds. We will bring into the discussion ideas and examples from human development and trauma psychology, world affairs, the Bible, and notable Church writers. Through these various perspectives we will deepen our understanding of how our attachments and attachment patterns bring joy or anxiety to our lives. Hopefully we will gain more insight into what we wish to foster or change in order to make our lives more balanced and joyful—with the joy that comes from trusting in God.

Foundation of attachment in infancy

IN THE FIELD OF HUMAN DEVELOPMENT "attachment" has a specialized meaning: the bond between small children and their caregivers such that children cling to these figures when frightened and seek them when in need. With that definition as a nucleus we will continue to conceptualize attachment more broadly.

Attachment begins in infancy. We spend our first three years within our family forming relationships and attachments, and from that phase we carry attachment patterns that influence us for the rest of our lives. This does not mean that our fate is sealed in those early years. No, but it means that life gives us the opportunity to become conscious of our attachment patterns and to choose what to foster and what to change.

During our early years, before we begin to master language, the right side of our brain is busy mastering fundamental relational patterns. Baby makes a face, mommy mirrors it back. They develop a conversational exchange based on facial expressions, gestures, touch, and sounds. Through this, they share their joy in each other's company, and mom or dad or grandma or big brother is able to comfort baby when baby is upset. Through this right brain to right brain communication the baby and caregiver form one mind in two bodies. Yes, one mind in two. The caregiver thus senses the infant's needs and modulates its feelings until it grows into fulfilling these functions for itself.

Thus the memories of our first years of life leave us, not with a story line, but with a basic sense that life is organized around certain kinds of people and relationships. There are the four basic attitudes that people carry away from the earliest years of life. We may expect to find safe and loving people whom we can turn to for help. No matter how difficult or dangerous life becomes, we can count on a "home base" of safe relationships. Or conversely, we may sense that people are basically preoccupied—wrapped up in their own worlds—and we have to look out for ourselves the best we can. Or again, we may believe that people are basically inconsistent and that we can never know what to expect. Sometimes they connect with us, sometimes they connect with who they want us to be, and sometimes they miss completely. Or again, we may come away from those early years sensing that no one can be trusted because the same people can be warm to us one moment, and frightening the next.

To summarize, we grow up expecting our close ones to help us, neglect us, confuse us, or frighten us. We will refer

back to these four attitudes as we go along. To use the metaphor of a dramatic production, these attitudes comprise the
backdrop and scenery against which the narrative of life later
unfolds.

Later attachment relationships

THE ATTACHMENTS AND BONDS we form in later life are largely
affected by our knowledge of what helps us feel better when
we are lonely, upset, frustrated, or ashamed. If we believe
close ones can be helpful, we may bond with a willing con-
versation partner based on the underlying belief that our
hurts can be transformed in the context of sharing. Some per-
sonalities bond with someone they can yell at or blame. According to their underlying belief, the surest route to relief is
to forcibly put the bad feelings into someone else as if the
other were a box or container. Others will eat, drink, or
smoke, in the belief that those are the most potent ways to
deal with distress. Others seek solitude, distraction, stimula-
tion, all based on their experience of what brings relief. Still
others will pray in the underlying belief that God is always
there to help us through every difficulty. We readily form
bonds with the source of our relief, even if that relief is not
reliable. Thus the emotional tone of our attachments may be
love, fear, gratification, debt, resentment, or some combination of feelings based on how we experience relief.

Our personal boundaries prevent us from just spontane-
ously bonding with anyone we meet. Attachments are often
formed in the context of shared, high-energy experiences. It
can be a moment of shared laughter or tears, the intensity of
the classroom experience or the battlefield, or the electrifying
experience of cheering the home team to victory or attending
a rock concert. We bond more easily when our feelings are
warmed up by sugar, caffeine, or alcohol, or when we are

simply worn down by fatigue. Any of these experiences can help shift us into a more right brain way of being in the world—into the right brain world of attachment formation.

What characterizes healthy patterns of human attachment? All the Gospel commandments concerning love for our neighbor show us the way. Healthy patterns are characterized by love, mutual respect, collaboration, and sharing life in a manner conducive to mutual salvation. We strive to appreciate other persons for who they really are and not just as roles, whether assigned by ourselves or by society.

Attachment roles

SOMETIMES IF WE OURSELVES are very attached to a certain role, we unwittingly invite others to take up reciprocal roles to aid us in playing out our own. For example, if we are attached to the role of caregiver, there is the danger of caring for other adults in such a way that they feel managed, treated as children. If we are attached to the role of being a victim, we may treat others as a threat even when they are trying to be kind. If parents are attached to the role of founding the "perfect family," they may deny other family members access to needed care. Moreover, if people are deeply involved in playing a certain role, they may recruit others to play roles that do not fit them at all, causing much distress. Their close ones may feel that a mask has been forced upon them and that their true self is stifled. Thus, bonding with a role sometimes gets in the way of bonding with people.

Other Dimensions of Attachment

Attachments between historical groups

I THINK THAT WE ALSO SEE bonds develop between social, political, or religious groups. This is certainly so if we look at attachment bonds in terms of emotional investments and reciprocal roles. In the Old Testament, for example, there was a bond between the Hebrew people and the Egyptians who enslaved them. The reciprocal roles were defined by the dynamics of subjugation. The Egyptians were emotionally invested in them out of fear—the Hebrews were becoming numerous and they feared that they would side with their enemies in a time of battle (Ex. 1:10). Out of their fear, they induced fear in their captives so that they would obey them. So there was a bond of mutual fear.

In the early days of Christianity, there was an attachment between the Jewish and Christian communities as they defined their identities in terms of one another. The Jewish people worshipped on Saturday, the Christian people on Sunday. The Pharisees fasted on Monday and Thursday, the Christians on Wednesday and Friday. Each group claimed the role of God's chosen people, while assigning the other to the role of being in error, a role resented on both sides. The emotional investment of the groups ranged from outright hostility to a desire to convert the other to the true faith as each one saw the truth. Even today, one faith cannot be defined without reference to the other.

In the Americas there are bonds between people groups also defined by history, complementary roles, and emotional

investment. This is true among Americans of European ances-
try, Native Americans, Afro-Americans, Spanish speaking
peoples and, to some degree, Asian Americans. For African
Americans, the historical role of enslaved worker carried with
it the emotional role of carrying shame. The historical role has
been easier to eliminate than the emotional role, based on the
mutual emotional investment of different people groups.
What would it take to adopt new emotional roles among the
races? As long as we as a nation are invested in earthly prosperity, status, and a comfortable life style, we will react with
suspicion and hostility to any people group we see as threat-
ening the good of our group, just as the ancient Egyptians felt
threatened by the Hebrew people. Only the Christ-loving spiritual path of humility, non-acquisitiveness, and love for our
neighbor can change the nature of inter-racial attachments.

Painful attachments

In honest communication, words and gesture are used in
the service of self-disclosure. Our most painful attachments,
however, are those that give us pleasure and pain through
manipulation of our feelings, our hopes, and our fears. When
I say manipulation I mean the use of language and gesture,
not for self-disclosure, but mechanically, to produce a desired effect. For example, an abusive husband says, "I love
you; I'll never do it again." The purpose of the statement is to
keep the wife from leaving the relationship. Thus he makes
up to her, giving her the feeling of relief; he raises her hopes
that this time it will last.

Manipulative bonds are different from bonds in which
we feel pain out of sympathy for the sufferings of another.
This is characteristic of the Christian bond in which we *Rejoice with those who are rejoicing. And weep with those who are
weeping* (Rm. 12:15). Underlying manipulative interactions is

the thought: I feel bad; no one really cares, so for relief I have to put my bad feelings on someone else. This results in yelling, blaming, and battering. The person who feels this way has learned it from experience, but they can still have corrective experiences. There is a different thought process underlying genuine intimacy: I feel bad; others are capable of sympathy and will voluntarily help me. This leads to sharing and honest communication.

Trauma bonds

AN INTERESTING FACET of human nature is that we tend to bond in times of crisis and danger. Thus soldiers bond with the men or women in their units. The Orthodox Christians under communism and the Ottoman Turks developed a great cohesion in their underground church movements. It is not unusual to read that when they finally gained their freedom, some longed for the closeness and the spiritual depth of the times of persecution. Fr. George Calciu, of blessed memory, shared about his life after liberation from the Romanian communist prison system:

> We had a kind of nostalgia about the prison. ... Because in prison we had the most spiritual life. We reached levels that we are not able to reach in this world. Isolated, anchored in Jesus Christ, we had joys and illuminations that this world cannot offer [Calciu, 1997, pp. 165–166].

The times of crisis strengthened their attachments to one another and their bonds with God.

Very strong bonds are fostered by dependency, especially if the one we depend on is sometimes kind and sometimes cruel. This fosters what some call a "trauma bond" or "betrayal bond." This is a factor in abusive family relationships—the alternation of affection and anger intensifies the bonds. These are bonds that foster intense anxiety and sorrows. The same

kind of bonding may happen in the case of captors and captives. There was a famous case in Stockholm, Sweden, where
women, who for political reasons were held hostage at a bank,
developed trauma bonds with their captors. Two of them wait-
ed for a full ten years—until their captors finished their prison
sentences—to marry them in a double ceremony attended by
fellow former hostages (Carnes, 1997, pp. 34–35).

Other examples of this trauma bonding include slaves to
their masters once the slaves have been "broken." "Breaking"
means systematically inducing the feeling that resistance is
futile. The intense loyalty of abused children to their parents
and abused women to their partners is characteristic of trauma
bonds, just as the Stockholm brides were loyal to their former
captors. This seems to be rooted in the most fundamental aspect of bonding: We bond to the ones who provide for us. If
the same person who provides for dependency needs—food,
shelter, clothing, and protection from outside threats—also
frightens us, our instincts give us conflicting messages to flee
from and cling to the same person. This results in feeling stuck
and helpless. Long after the danger is over the feeling may lin-
ger, but God provides us options for healing. *I have strength for
anything in Christ who empowers me* (Php. 4:13, author's translation).

In abusive relationships it often seems that for one person
to win, the other has to lose; for one to have self-esteem, the
other must be humiliated; for one to feel good, the other must
swallow all the badness. Without a strong attachment, the
abused one might simply walk away and let the abuse be a one-
or two-time event. But within the grip of a trauma bond, the
abuser and the abuse sufferer are addicted to one another.

I do not use the word addicted lightly, because in all addictions highs and lows alternate from the same source: People
who gamble both win and lose; people with chemical addictions turn to the same toxin that makes them ill in order to feel

better. Sometimes for a person to break free, the lows have to dominate the highs to such an extent that the cycle of addiction crumbles.

Bonds mediated by struggle

WITHOUT THE INTENSITY OF TRAUMA, there are other bonds that are mediated by voluntarily accepted struggles. Perhaps these bonds are strengthened by an aspect of human nature: We value the things and the relationships for which we pay or sacrifice or suffer. Students are proud of the rigor of their school. Mothers' love is deepened by the struggles of pregnancy and childbirth. *When a woman is in labor she is in distress, for her time has come. Yet when she has given birth to her child, she no longer remembers the agony for the joy of having brought a human into the world* (Jn. 16:21). Perhaps the agony is not so much forgotten as it is transmuted into a bond—the mother and child have come through a life-and-death struggle together that heightens the value of the new life in her heart.

The value of Orthodox baptism is in the bond it fosters with Jesus Christ—what earthly joy can compare with being close to the Lord? When I look back on my own group baptismal experience decades ago, I cherish the memory of the icy river in which we were immersed on that early spring day. The bitterness of the weather seems to embellish the joy I have in belonging to the Church. Of course that is a small thing, an almost foolish thing, compared to the deeper spiritual realities. But the beauty of our faith is that it is a fully embodied faith and the various sensory impressions that we receive as part of our worship help form the soul in devoutness.

Intra-psychic attachments

THERE IS A NEED for healthy attachments within the human psyche as well. "It is necessary in the first instance to love God," says St. Pavel Florensky, for "without love the personality is broken up into a multitude of fragmentary psychological moments and elements. The love of God is that which holds the personality together" (1987, p. 27). I have learned through clinical work that there are people who suffer inner division not from overt trauma, but through neglect and lack of love. We desperately need love to bind our internal parts together.

According to the 11th century *Philokalia* author, St. Nikitas, we must labor to restore the faculties of the soul to the healthy state in which God first created them. For this, repentance and spiritual struggle are necessary, otherwise "our soul will be divided against itself and because of the turbulence of its powers will remain impervious to the rays of the Spirit" (vol. 4, p. 83).

This same author asserts that through the turbulence of the warring passions—that is, emotions, desires, and attitudes—a person develops "multifarious self-antagonistic parts." Lacking the inner cohesion supplied by God's love, such a person becomes hostile. Thus the inner chaos is reflected in abusive or manipulative attachment patterns with others.

> If when aroused and active a man's [indignation, desire, and thought] spontaneously operate in accordance with nature, they make him godlike and divine, sound in his actions and never in any way dislodged from nature's bedrock. But if, betraying his own nature, he follows a course that is contrary to nature, these same powers will turn him... into a polymorphic monster, compounded of many self-antagonistic parts [*Philokalia*, vol. 4, pp. 82–83].

St. Nikitas implicitly contrasts this to the original state of human nature, created to be in God's image as a unity of harmonious parts. Souls lacking closeness to God have strong attachments to pleasures that lie in the flesh and the ego—that is, to self-gratification—and a weak attachment to the spiritual heart, designed to be the innermost nucleus of the human person, mediating the harmony of the whole through internal bonds of love. In the original Greek of the Gospels, this inner heart is called the *nous*.

This same author, as translated in the Philokalia, actually speaks of addictions to our passions, in much the same way that we now speak of addictions to substances and behaviors. But he also speaks of addiction to fickle human praise, something that society does not detect as problematic. In fact society encourages us to seek this praise as a high good.

Fr. Zacharias, heir to the spiritual inheritance of St. Sophrony and St. Silouan of Mount Athos, shares a powerful way to help the soul rediscover its God-given pattern of inner connectedness. We need to remember that we were created for more than this present, passing world and so make the attempt to remember and prepare for the hour of our death.

> Mindfulness of death is evidently stronger than any passionate attachment, and the mind is now free to descend into the heart and unite with it. This discovery of the heart is the beginning of man's salvation [Zacharou, 2008, p. 21].

Attachment to thoughts and impulses

IN OUR PRE-REFLECTIVE STATE, we tend to be bonded to the thoughts and impulses that arise within ourselves. These thoughts and impulses can even seem to comprise who we are. As we advance in spiritual struggle, we learn to challenge that belief and to begin to see thoughts and impulses as visitors that we may welcome or dismiss after discerning their nature. Orthodox spiritual tradition is not alone in addressing our inner ordering: Some therapeutic models are designed to help people separate their core self from the thoughts and impulses that cause them grief.

Narrative therapy, for example helps people separate the "voice" of anorexia or alcohol or drugs from their own authentic voice. People may, through writing letters to their addiction, discover how addiction has been a powerful attachment figure, replacing human and divine relationships. Through journaling on how alcohol prompts them to drink they may learn to distance from the feeling that "I" want a drink. They are free to discover a sense of "I-ness" that is separate from their impulses.

There are other models that allow people, in a manner similar to what I just outlined, to also distance from their fears, anger, and other difficult emotions by stepping out from behind the feelings, as it were, to discover their spiritual core which is not blown about by the winds of strong emotion.[1]

---

[1] For example: Internal Family Systems Therapy (IFS) developed by Richard Schwartz. (See https://ifs-institute.com/.) Also the Dynamic Needs Meeting Strategy (DNMS) developed by Shirley Jean Schmidt. (See https://www.dnmsinstitute.com/home/.)

Spiritual Life

Just as we find in our social relations that intense, shared experiences can foster bonding, so it is in our spiritual life. Intensely felt need or intense fear draws us into intense prayer. God hears these prayers and it bonds us more deeply to Him. Thus the very experiences that we least value, that may lead us to question God for allowing them to happen, can be of value to us as they become catalysts for prayer. It is with the same hope of drawing closer to God that we undertake fasting, simplicity of living, and voluntary hardships. When we look at the media-driven culture around us it is abundantly evident that the sated existence that the world calls life extinguishes the spiritual spark.

There are examples in Scripture of intense longing begetting intense prayer and closeness to the Lord. One is the childless couple Zechariah and Elizabeth. The fruit of their patience was both the deepening of their own spiritual life and the birth of John the Baptist. The *Protoevangelium* of James tells a parallel story, not in the Bible, about the childlessness of Joachim and Anna. They, too, nearly reached the point of despair before their prayer was heard, but then God worked out their own sanctification through the birth of the Virgin Mary.

Now from the sublime to the mundane: Here is an example from my own life. A highway experience once brought me to a crescendo of desperation and fear. I was driving in the center lane on the interstate when my accelerator stopped working. Cars were passing me on both sides leaving me no escape route. The prayer that I cried out then, from the soles of my feet to the hairs of my head, has now become for me the touchstone of prayer. Needless to say, God heard me, because I am here to tell the story. I cannot say how many times I have gone back to that moment to get in touch with the reality of heartfelt prayer. In a similar vein, I know parents with special stories about praying for their children—children, one way or another, lead many parents to the depths of prayer. Thus, while attachment bonds can be the root of our deepest angst and distress, that same distress can also be the root of our deepening attachment to God.

Spiritual images and bonding

FOR HUMAN BEINGS to bond with God, the Son of God had first to come as a little baby so that He could bond with our humanity. The Serbian Orthodox have the endearing tradition of calling Christmas the feast of "Božić" which translates as the feast of "the Little God," "Goddy" if you will. Before being introduced to Christ they worshipped fierce, adult gods. They were so deeply moved by hearing of the tender, loving Baby God, that it was easy for them to become attached to Him. When we see the icons of the Virgin caressing the Baby God, it awakens the childlike parts of us that know how to form a loving attachment and this draws us closer to God.

When we pray with icons, not only do we communicate our love and regard for the persons depicted on them, but we begin to draw their holy gestures and attitudes within our souls so that we may begin to imitate them. In speaking of holy icons that have faded with time, St. Paisios of Mount Athos once said in a poetic vein:

> When someone venerates the holy Icons with devoutness and fervent love, he absorbs the colours from them and the Saints

are imprinted on his soul. The Saints are pleased when they are lifted up from the paper or the wood and imprinted in people's hearts [St. Paisios, 2008, p. 164].

As I said earlier, to cling to an attachment figure when frightened or in danger is God-given and instinctive. The holy icons of the Orthodox Church show the Baby Jesus clinging to His Mother. I am thinking now of an icon that is very famous both in the Eastern Orthodox and the Roman Catholic Church. In the former it is known as The Virgin of the Passion; in the latter, as Our Lady of Perpetual Help. In this image the Child Jesus has been frightened by the appearance, in the upper corners of the composition, of two angels carrying the cross, the lance, and the spear. He has just leapt into His Mother's arms, holding on to her right hand with both His small hands. One sandal has come untied and dangles from His foot because of His haste in running to her. His bond with His Mother is secure and a source of joy to both of them as well as a source of hope to us.

Some thirty years later at the time of His Crucifixion, the Lord Jesus again demonstrates the strength of His attachment to His Mother, but this time the roles are reversed as He cares for her in the midst of His agony:

> When Jesus saw his mother and the disciple whom he loved standing there, he said to his mother, "Woman, here is your son." Then he said to the disciple, "Here is your mother." And from that hour the disciple took her into his own home [Jn. 19:26–27].

He cares for them both by forming a new bond between them. And through that gesture, by extension, He bids us all to develop lasting bonds with her and to take her into our hearts and homes.

Healthier attachments through spiritual life

WHEN WE GIVE OUR LIVES TO GOD, especially in Holy Baptism, we call this spiritual rebirth. *What is born of the flesh is flesh, and what is born of the Spirit is spirit* (Jn. 3:6).

> To all who received him, to those believing in his name, he gave authority to become God's children, who were born, not merely in a physical sense, or from a fleshly impulse, or from man's desire, but of God [Jn. 1:12–13].

Throughout this time of rebirth, we renegotiate our attachments. Over time we work to make our primary attachment to God and also to order all our relationships to created things in Him, through Him, and for Him. For example, if we suffer from emotional eating—eating to soothe troubled emotions rather than for physical need—we have an attachment to food, an attachment that causes a mixture of gratification and trouble. As we begin to renegotiate our attachments we begin to move toward using food to strengthen our bond with God, remembering that He provided the food for us and thanking Him for it. We also have the potent medicine of the Holy Eucharist, in which we eat the Body and Blood of our Lord Jesus Christ. Until we have tasted true consolation in Him, how can we weaken our attachments to passing ones?

This transformation is not easy and it does not happen overnight. But we can have as our goal to attach ourselves more and more firmly to the only One who can give us lasting comfort and consolation, while loosening the addictive bonds that cause us so much sorrow. Our Lord,

> calling a little child forward… had him stand in the midst of them. Then he said, "Truly I tell you, unless you change and become like little children, you will never enter the kingdom of heaven. Whoever, then, humbles himself as this little child is the greatest in the kingdom of heaven [Mt. 18: 2–4].

When we access our childlike parts we can form new bonding patterns, withdrawing our vital energy from harmful attachments and strengthening our bonds with the Lord.

In the early centuries of the Christian faith, there was emphasis on leaving behind family attachments to follow Christ. The first-called apostles, for example, Peter, Andrew, James, and John were fishermen. When the Lord Jesus called, they left their boats, their nets, and their families in order to follow Him. Simon the Zealot—the bridegroom of the Cana wedding—left his bride. Matthew left his employment collecting taxes. These men had all been embedded in society by the customary ties that root people and give their lives meaning in the world. Christ called them from the normal and expected to something beyond this world.

In our times many people suffer from a poverty of meaningful attachments. Rather than calling us to give up attachments for His sake, Jesus may be leading us to heal through developing healthy attachments. Speaking to a community of nuns St. Paisios says: "Cultivate love, the spiritual kind. You should love one another like a mother loves her child. You should have a sense of [sister]hood and spiritual sacrifice" (St. Paisios, 2008, p. 134). To the lay people he says that it is important to

> maintain relationships with friends and relatives who live a spiritual life so that they will be helped. The Christian who is struggling in the world is helped when he has relationships with spiritual people [p. 134].

The one who does not love the brother whom he has seen cannot love God whom he has not seen (I Jn. 4:20b).

Dialogue

HAVING LOOKED AT ATTACHMENT from different angles, it becomes apparent that the Eastern Church and the psychological disciplines look at it in only partially overlapping ways. The Church often uses the term "attachment" in a negative sense, using "love" or similar words for positive bonds. The Church is primarily concerned with the objects of our attachments, and also with their nature: Are they attachments of self-gratification or bonds of love?

The Orthodox Faith urges us to invest our souls in our relationship with God, and to enter into other relationships in and through Him. This is in harmony with the biblical verse: *But first of all seek God's kingdom and his righteousness, and all these things will be provided for you as well* (Mt. 6:33).

The psychological disciplines concern themselves primarily with the quality of our attachments to early caregivers and also with how those patterns impact our later attachments to other people, behaviors, objects, and substances. It is a given that attachment first happens with our parents or early caregivers; thus the question of appropriate objects of attachment comes later in life. Only then is there the potential to use food, spending, sex, substances, material objects, or electronic pastimes to fill our deep relational needs.

Shared concerns

THUS OUR TWO FRAMES of reference, although using different vocabularies and different standards of health, share a concern about what the Church would call attachments of self-gratification versus bonds of love, while psychology might call these unhealthy versus healthy attachments.

A second potential point of shared concern is how the quality of our attachments with early caregivers affects the way we approach God, or even whether or not we wish to approach God. Ana-Maria Rizzuto, a Roman Catholic analyst, has done years of research on how people form a conception of what God is like. She calls these conceptions "God images," differentiating these from Who God is in Himself. She came up with four basic attitudes people may have toward God: First, "He loves me and I love Him"; second, "I'm not really sure if He exists"; third, "He exists, but I'm not sure how much it matters to me"; and finally, "He exists and He is persecuting me" (Rizzuto, 1979). These four attitudes seem to parallel the four basic attachment patterns that people develop in childhood: first, attachment based on security and love from the parents or caregivers; second, attachment with parents who are neglectful and not really "there"; third, attachment with parents who are inconsistent in responding to their child; and fourth, attachment with abusive or frightening parents.

While I have not yet come across passages in the early Church writers conveying the sense of God images or attachment to them, a present-day bishop, Metropolitan Athanasios of Cyprus, has remarked that "People may think of themselves as devout Christians but their notions of Christ may have no relevance to Christ" (Markides, 2001, p. 75). He attributes this primarily to forming opinions in the absence of genuine spiritual guidance. Those opinions could certainly be influenced by early experiences, but he does not comment.

There may well be a relationship between the early attachment patterns and later beliefs and attitudes toward God, but it is not simply cause and effect, because we grow up with relationships and attachments to different people; we may have corrective or harmful experiences as we get older, we are affected by the culture around us, and so on. We also have to take into account the many ways that God reaches out to us, as well as our own free will. Because of the many factors involved, people may experience God differently at different points of their lives. This variety of personal—and group—experience of God is, in fact, reflected in spiritual texts and in the Scriptures.

Scriptural themes

THERE ARE WRITERS who speak of our struggle against personal, inherited, and ancestral sin. Inherited sin refers to how the shortcomings of our parents and forebears have a negative impact on us, an idea that certainly encompasses difficult attachment patterns. In addition, the Scriptures, Church services, and texts on spiritual life are full of the themes of trust, doubt, ambivalence, and wrestling with God—themes which can be distilled from the forgoing discussion of God images. These are momentous themes, major life themes that are sometimes embodied in individuals, sometimes in people groups, and sometimes presented as experiences that figures pass through.

Church literature is much more organic and poetic in its approach than the systematized four types that I presented from psychology. A handful of examples—Moses is a figure of faith; in the Exodus, the Hebrew people were figures of doubt when they worshipped the golden calf, and they were figures of ambivalence when they murmured, wishing to turn back; Jacob and Job both wrestled—the first with an angel and the second with God. Through this last example we see that the experience of wrestling with God is not a negative thing. In fact according to Elder Aimilianos, it is a necessary part of the spiritual path (2005, p. 16 ff.).

When the Scriptures hold up images of these different attitudes toward God they invite us to reflect on them as experiences that any of us may embody at different times. They are multi-layered, more than the psychological frames of reference. In the spiritual view, beyond the family influence on the human person, free will is an indispensable part of human nature; there are spiritual forces of good and evil, all at work simultaneously.

Conclusion

FINALLY THEN, at the root of our deepest joys and anxieties we find both our attachment heritage and our attachment choices; we find both the objects and the patterns of our attachment. This is an area where growth and healing are possible throughout our lifetime. If our family has given us an inheritance of positive attachment patterns we still make the choice to adopt or reject them. If our family has given us an inheritance of destructive attachment patterns, let that be a cause for courage, because in either case our lives are weighed, not by what we once were given, but by what we now do with it. If we take inventory and see the need for improvement, we can foster change within ourselves, among our relationships, and even among our races and nations. We have sources of help in this world and beyond this world. I firmly believe that in Christ Jesus we are here to be heroes; *in all these things we are completely victorious through the one who loved us* (Rom. 8:37). Our struggles are the raw material of that heroism.

References and Bibliography
Second Essay

Aimilianos, (Archimandrite). (2005). *The Church at prayer: the mystical liturgy of the heart.* (The Holy Convent of the Annunciation, Ormylia, Eds.). Athens: Indiktos.

Berlin, Adele & Brettler, Mark Z., (Eds.) and Fishbane, Michael (Consulting Ed.). (2004). *The Jewish study Bible.* New York: Oxford University.

Calciu, (Priest) George. (1997). *Christ is calling you! A course in catacomb pastorship.* Platina, CA: St. Herman of Alaska Brotherhood.

Carnes, Patrick. (1997). *The betrayal bond: breaking free of exploitive relationships.* Deerfield Beach, FL: Health Communications, Inc.

Danker, Frederick W., (Ed.). (2000). *A Greek-English lexicon of the New Testament and other early Christian Literature,* (3rd ed.). Chicago: The University of Chicago.

Fonagy, Peter, Gergely, György, Jurist, Elliot & Target, Mary. (2004). *Affect regulation, mentalization, and the development of the self.* New York: Other.

Holy Apostles Convent. (2003). *The Orthodox New Testament, Vol. 2: Acts, Epistles, and Revelation.* Buena Vista, CO: Holy Apostles Convent and Dormition Skete.

John Climacus, St. (c. 649/1991). *The ladder of divine ascent.* (Revised ed.), (A. L. Moore and Holy Transfiguration Monastery, Trans.). Brookline, MA: Holy Transfiguration Monastery.

Lampe, G. W. H., (Ed.). (1968). *A patristic Greek lexicon.* Oxford: The University Press, Oxford.

Markides, Kyriakos. (2001). *The mountain of silence: A search for Orthodox spirituality.* New York, NY: Image.

Mary, (Mother) & Ware, (Archimandrite) Kallistos, (Trans.). (1978/ 2002). *The Lenten triodion.* South Canaan, PA: St. Tikhon's Seminary.

McLean Hospital. (2000). McLean researchers document brain damage linked to child abuse and neglect. Retrieved from: www. mclean.harvard.edu.PublicAffairs/20001214_child_abuse.htm.

Migne, J.-P., (Ed.). (1857–1866). *Patrologiæ Græcæ,* vol. 62. Paris: Migne.

Nikitas Stithatos, St. (11th cent./1995). On the practice of the virtues. In G. E. H. Palmer, P. Sherrard, & K. Ware, (Trans. and Eds.), *The philokalia,* vol. 4 (pp. 79–106). London: Faber and Faber Ltd.

Oden, Thomas C., (Gen. Ed.). (1999). *Ancient Christian commentary on Scripture. New Testament,* vol. 8, (M. J. Edwards, Ed.). Downers Grove, IL: InterVarsity.

Paisios the New, St. (2008). *Spiritual counsels,* vol. II: *Spiritual awakening,* (Fr. P. Chamberas, Trans., A. Famellos & A. Masters, Eds.). Thessaloniki, Greece: Holy Monastery "Evangelist John the Theologian."

Palmer, G. E. H., Sherrard, Philip, & Ware, Kallistos, (Trans. and Eds.). (1979–1995). *The philokalia,* vols. 1–4. London: Faber and Faber Ltd.

Pavel Florensky, St. (1987). *Salt of the earth or a narrative on the life of the elder of Gethsemane Skete Hieromonk Abba Isadore,* (R. Betts, Trans., St. Herman B'hood, Eds.). Platina, CA: St. Herman of Alaska Brotherhood.

Reardon, (Priest) Patrick H. (2000). *Christ in the Psalms.* Ben Lomond, CA: Conciliar.

Rizzuto, Ana-Maria. (1979). *The birth of the living God.* Chicago: The University of Chicago.

Rose, (Hieromonk) Seraphim, (Trans.). (1996). *Little Russian philo-kalia*, vol. 1: *Saint Seraphim of Sarov*. Platina, CA: St. Herman of Alaska Brotherhood.

Schaff, Philip, (Ed.). (1979). *A select library of the Nicene and post-Nicene Fathers of the Christian Church*, series 1, vol. 13. Saint Chrysostom, *Homilies on Ephesians* XI, pp. 102 – 108. Grand Rapids, MI: Wm B. Eerdmans.

Schwartz, Richard C. (1995). *Internal family systems therapy*. New York: Guilford.

Shartz, (Monk) Cosmas. (2010). Love without exceptions: delivered at the 17th annual Brotherhood of St. Moses the Black Conference, Anniston, AL, May 14, 2010. From a forthcoming book.

Siegel, Daniel J. (2009). Google Personal Growth Series: Mindsight: The New Science of Personal Transformation. Retrieved June 8, 2009 from: http://www.youtube.com/watch?v=Gr4Od7kqDT8.

Strong, James. (1890/1973). *The exhaustive concordance of the Bible*. New York: Abingdon.

Thurman, Howard. (1965). *The luminous darkness: A personal interpretation of the anatomy of segregation and the ground of hope*. New York: Harper & Row.

Trench, Richard C. (1876/2000). *Trench's synonyms of the New Testament*. Peabody, MA: Hendrickson Publishers, Inc.

Wallin, David J. (2007). *Attachment in psychotherapy*. New York: Guilford.

Wigram, George V. (1860). *The Englishman's Hebrew and Chaldee concordance of the Old Testament*, 2nd ed, revised. London: Walton and Maberly.

_____. (1903/2006). *The Englishman's Greek concordance of the New Testament*. Peabody, MA: Hendrickson.

Zacharou, (Archimandrite) Zacharias. (2008). *The hidden man of the heart (1 Peter 3:4): the cultivation of the heart in Orthodox Christian anthropology*. Waymart, PA: Mount Thabor.

Third Essay, 2018:
Gratitude:
The Fruit of Trust

In everything give thanks:
for this is the will of God in Christ Jesus
concerning you (I Th. 5:18).
Giving thanks always for all things unto God, even the Father,
in the name of our Lord Jesus Christ
(Eph. 5:20).

GRATITUDE AND THANKSGIVING are such very basic experiences that even comprehensive dictionaries define one by the other. Gratitude is a warmhearted recognition of favors received and the disposition to acknowledge them. "Gratitude" is also a buzz word in psychotherapy, coming in from Buddhist psychology. Medically speaking, gratitude does wonders for the brain and, indeed, the whole body; in fact even functional brain scans can differentiate when a research subject enters a grateful state of mind. So gratitude has social, psychological and medical aspects.

But for us, as Orthodox Christians seeking the Kingdom of Heaven, gratitude is much, much more. In order for us to plumb the riches of gratitude we will need faithful guides: In addition to St. Paul we will recruit others including St. Paisios of Mount Athos, St. Nikolai Velimirović, and St. Anthony the Great. We will ask these guides to show us how gratitude is the fruit of trust and how, in offering thanks and praise to God, we can draw closer to Him and to one another.

Impediments to gratitude

To ALWAYS GIVE THANKS—this is such a clear and straightforward counsel from the Scriptures yet, in my experience, people often find this very difficult—it doesn't resonate with how they know life. Suggesting gratitude may elicit eye-rolling or the emotional equivalent. It may elicit the exasperated feeling of being misunderstood by someone who should know better. So this phenomenon has naturally come to pique my interest—why is this deceptively light commandment so difficult for people? And how do we get past the difficulty ourselves or help others? For this question we will pursue both psychological and spiritual answers.

So what are the impediments? I see two areas to consider: first, the thoughts and feelings we have pertaining to gratitude itself and, second, understanding what the Scriptures are asking of us. So let's begin with the human and psychological component: What are the thoughts that impede us from gratitude toward God? A big one is the genuine comfort of taking good things for granted. Any time we give thanks we are implicitly acknowledging that life is fragile and that the gifts that have been given us could, like Job's, be removed when we least expect it. So as we approach gratitude, it may spark a bit of anxiety that could deter us from going deeper.

An important aspect of taking things for granted is the thought of normalcy—what we have is within the norms of society or, perhaps, even less than the "average" person. So these blessings don't inspire recognition because they just seem natural, or because they are mediated by human ingenuity and technology. How often do we wash our face in the morning and give thanks to God for the blessing of running water, or for safe water? Perhaps Flint, Michigan, with its lead-laced waters shifted our perception of this.

Very close to these thoughts is the thought of entitlement: We may believe that we are basically good people and so deserve good things in this life. We don't give thanks for the things that we have earned; they are our due. We expect them and have a right to them. This brings to mind, naturally, the Lord's words about service: *So you likewise, when you have done all those things commanded you, say, We are unprofitable servants: we have done our duty* (Lk. 17:10). These words, taken to heart, are an antidote to entitlement. When we remember that the good we have done is a duty, then the good things we experience are no longer our wages, but grace-filled blessings for which we should offer thanks.

The opposite thought can also impede gratitude. If the verse *we are unprofitable servants* seems to confirm thoughts of personal worthlessness, then we may wonder: Why would God bother with me? Why would He consider my needs and prayers? Thus good things we experience are rendered random and meaningless. Or worse, they are portents that something bad is about to happen on the heels of the good. But they are not appreciated as respite moments from God.

In short, gratitude toward God requires humility. The virtues, in a classical understanding, are the optimal balance point between extremes. As such, humility lies not in extreme self-abasement or in self-exaltation. Humility, as a wise man observed, serves to take the focus away from self entirely (see Hammarskjöld, 1959/2006) so that we are free to unite ourselves to Christ.

Emotional obstacles

WE MAY ALSO FACE SIGNIFICANT obstacles in our moods and emotions that impede gratitude, especially depression and anxiety. These hinder thanksgiving in different ways: A thoughtful Christian writer, who was subject to bouts of depression, noticed this first warning sign of a depressive ep-isode: He stopped feeling grateful for everyday blessings such as his wife's care for him. There might not yet be any other symptoms—he didn't feel sad or irritable or tired—he just stopped feeling gratitude (see Roccas, 2017, p. 140). In the grips of a depression, a person is robbed of satisfaction in past accomplishment, present effectiveness, and future hope.

Depressed people often feel guilty for everything; thus, as Orthodox Christians, it is important to differentiate the spiritual from the physical aspects of this condition. Here are illustrations that may help: Perhaps we are primarily deject-ed because God's will in our lives seems too hard to ac-cept—we have the trajectory of our well-being plotted out, and life is not cooperating. If and when we become aware of such a power struggle with Providence, we should bring this to our confessor. That power struggle may mean that we have faith in a limited God—believing that He cannot use the present situation toward our good.

If, however, we are feeling low, combined with poor sleep, poor concentration, changes in appetite, then biological causes need to be ruled out. By biological causes I mean things such as chronic stress, inflammation, toxins, or even the side effects of some 200 commonly prescribed medica-tions. In clinical depression, often a completely reversible condition, the neurons themselves become sickly; therefore the medicines of repentance and confession, while necessary for our ongoing spiritual health, should not be the only means used to treat it.

Anxiety, on the other hand, is a state of over activation of survival systems in the brain. In this case, approaching grati-tude may sometimes help to calm it. When I say approaching gratitude, I mean the mental search for some object of grati-tude, even if we come up blank. Or if we can think of a grati-tude list, even without accessing the feeling of gratefulness, it can move us in the right direction, in combination with calming activities such as breathing deeply, drinking some water, or a soothing physical activity.

While anxiety is sometimes the result of personal sin and a guilty conscience, there are also various factors that leave a person vulnerable to anxiety. These include a genetic predisposition, being brought up by anxious parents, or growing up with trauma or chronic stressors. These factors also include issues with the processing of sensory information, which can leave a person feeling chronically overwhelmed. In all such cases we need to learn to calm the survival parts of the brain. Since gratitude includes the belief that something has enhanced our well-being, it is hard to feel grateful and threatened at the same time. But, as I stated above, moving our thoughts toward gratitude can be a first step toward reducing anxiety. And reducing anxiety, by whatever means, can also be a step toward gratitude.

Gratitude in the Orthodox Faith

NOW THAT WE HAVE EXAMINED some of the human impediments to gratitude, let us delve deeper into a biblical understanding of gratitude. Returning to St. Paul's letter to the Ephesians, let's begin a few verses earlier to establish the context:

> Watch then that you walk circumspectly, not as fools, but as wise, redeeming the present moment because the days are evil. Wherefore, do not be unwise, but discern the will of God. And do not be drunk with wine, in which is profligacy, but be filled with the Spirit; speaking to one another in psalms and hymns and spiritual songs, singing and making melody in your heart to the Lord; giving thanks always for everything in the name of our Lord Jesus Christ, to God, even the Father [Eph. 5:15–20].

So we see that the injunction to give thanks is given in the context of "evil days." And thanksgiving is offered as an antidote to drunkenness. When we are enjoying time with friends, or even sunk in despondency together, we should not get intoxicated with wine, or food, or sensual indulgence, but sing God's praises instead. St. Paul is not suggesting that praise and thanksgiving should eclipse the other established forms of prayer—offering petitions, offering repentance, and asking for deliverance—rather, praise and thanksgiving undergird the others. For if our God is not trustworthy and praiseworthy, why do we approach Him with petitions, repentance, and pleas for deliverance? Therefore, praise and thanksgiving are primary expressions of faith itself.

Why do I put praise and thanksgiving together? Here is a little clue from the Slavic languages: the word *hvala* is commonly used to show appreciation for some favor, just as we use "thanks" in English. But the word actually means "praise" in both Serbian and Church Slavonic. The implication is "I praise you for what you have done for me." Similarly *slava Bogu* is often rendered "thank God." It literally means "glory to God." These observations point to a deep connection between thanks, praise, and glory.

Now moving from Slavic roots to Greek ones: *Efharisteō,* "to offer thanks," "to offer prayers of thanksgiving," is a cognate of the word *efharistia,* from which we get our English "Eucharist." The prefix, *ef-* or *eu-,* means "well" and the root, *haris,* means "grace, favor, goodwill, gift, thanks, kindness" (Trenchard, 1998, p. 121). Someone who receives abundant grace, favor, or gifts would reciprocate. Notice how the gift giver, the gift, and the recipient are all contained in the language of gratitude. In a faith-centered life, someone who *recognizes* heavenly blessings would render thanks to God. Thus we see that spiritual gratitude establishes a three-way relationship between us, our heavenly Benefactor, and the attribute, gift, or thing that we are grateful for.

This gratitude triangle makes sense linguistically, but is it supported scripturally? Yes—of the nine letters of St. Paul to the Christians of various cities, eight begin with a thanksgiving right after the salutation. In one, he gives thanks to God for His encouragement and blessings towards them. In the others, remembering the faithful in his prayers, he gives thanks for their grace, faith, fellowship, and love. Perhaps the most eloquent is in First Thessalonians: *Remembering without ceasing your work of faith, and labor of love, and patience of hope* (1:3). In the passages where he gives thanks, the triangle is between Paul, God, and the virtues embodied in the local congregations.

As I was contemplating these matters, I came upon an article on spiritual joy and worldly joy or pleasure that parallels, and gives a foundation to, my observations on gratitude. The writer contrasts secular and spiritual definitions of joy: In the secular sense, joy is an emotional response to something whereas in the spiritual sense, joy is a relational response to Someone. Joy is our "disposition toward God." It is able to coexist with suffering, to blossom in the midst of it. This, he asserts, is because joy is less about emotion and more about belief. Joy is not self-complacent, ignoring or dismissing pain in our own lives, the lives of others, or in society at large. "Rather it goes deeper, seeing confidence in God—and for Christians, in Jesus Christ—as the reason for joy and a constant source of joy" (Martin, 2018, pp. 46-47).

Joy is foundational to gratitude—in Greek these are also cognate words: *Hara* means "joy" and *haris* means "thanks." In offering thanks we rejoice in God's goodness and providence. In order to be grateful, we have to be able to rejoice—to celebrate. This is different from the happiness that comes from pleasure or amusement.

Thus we see, through the above contemplation, that both joy and gratitude are relational. Christian joy focuses our attention on a relational line between God and us; gratitude focuses on the relational triangle of God, us, and His gifts. Spiritual gratitude is not just a matter of a gratitude list, as useful as those may be. It is not a list of the things that we have judged to be good in our lives. It is certainly not a tortured exercise of finding some minute thing to be grateful for in the midst of tragedy or overwhelming difficulty. So if offering thanks is not primarily an exercise in hunting for something to be grateful for, what is it? It is a practice of recognizing, trusting in the continual presence of God and His providential care, and of offering thanks for His goodness.

As I mentioned above, if we erroneously believe that gratitude is more about the gift than the giver, that error becomes a major impediment to rendering thanks. It spawns many ungrateful thoughts. "I was abused. I'm not giving thanks for that." "I have a low-paying job ... " or "I have no job— I'm not giving thanks for that." So how do we give thanks in trying situations?

In a memorable passage from *The Hiding Place* (1971), Corrie ten Boom describes a moment with her sister, Betsy, in the Nazi prison camp. There were fleas in the women's dorm; Corrie said there was no way she could imagine giving thanks for fleas. Betsy said, on faith, they had to do it. As it turned out, because of the fleas, the guards left the dorm room alone; the sisters were free to have worship services and Bible reading.

I love that story, and the fact that in the midst of their trials, they could have a sisterly argument over gratitude. On one level, it was not that important to give thanks for the fleas *per se*; it would have taken character just to give thanks to God for supporting and upholding them in their trials. But perhaps Betsy intuited that giving thanks for the pests was a creative act that could change their presence from a scourge to a blessing. We can't all be like Betsy: While the triangle of gratitude does require something to be grateful for, that something may be as simple and powerful as the strength for the present moment.

When Christ gives thanks

To DEEPEN OUR UNDERSTANDING of gratitude, let us visit the Bible passages where Christ gives thanks over loaves of bread. All four of the Gospels make mention of at least one time when our Lord multiplied loaves, and sometimes fish, for the thousands who came out into remote places to hear Him teach. Some verses say that He gave thanks; others say He looked up into heaven and blessed. We may not know the exact words He said, but the traditional Hebrew blessings begin with "Blessed art Thou, O LORD our God, King of the universe ... ." Those ancient prayers begin by blessing God, so each is called a blessing, while the whole prayer is one of praise and thanksgiving (Smith, 1983, p. 101). And so it makes sense if the evangelists used "giving thanks" and "blessing" interchangeably. As Matthew, Mark, and Luke narrate the Last Supper, they also say that our Lord took bread and blessed it. And He took the cup and gave thanks. But in all these instances, what happens next? A creative act! A miracle! The fish and loaves, or loaves and wine are multiplied: the first, to feed the stomachs of the multitudes; the second, to feed the souls of the faithful to this very day.

What would have happened if Jesus Christ had looked at the paltry quantity of bread and fish with mere earthly logic? It seems almost blasphemous to suggest such a possibility, but our purpose is not to detract from, but to better appreciate, His glory. So hypothetically, if Christ had used only an earthly calculus, then the food would barely have been enough for Him and the apostles. No crowds of thousands would have been fed. Perhaps some, indeed, would have fainted on the way home. And the bread and wine would not have been transformed into His divine Body and Blood to nourish the faithful. The Faith, as we know it, would not exist if Jesus looked at challenges facing Him with a limited, rational perspective.

So I ask you, when our Lord gave thanks to the Father, was that a creative act only because He, the Son of God, uttered the prayer? Or is there something inherently creative about rendering thanks to God? I have gradually come to understand the latter, that praising God is intrinsically a creative act. Or, more accurately, God Himself is the Creator; giving thanks opens us up to His creative intervention in our lives. As an experienced spiritual father once liked to say, "If you give thanks for everything that happens to you, it opens the doors of God's Providence to you."

God is merciful and loves us and wants to help us. Giving thanks opens our hearts just as we open our hands up to receive a material gift. We may say that we want His help, but if we let our rational, evaluative, judgmental mind get the upper hand, it's like praying without realizing that our fists are tightly clenched. God is right there saying, "My child, I have here the answer to your prayer, but I'm not going to hurt your fingers to give it to you!" Then when we receive nothing, we get mad at God and end up judging Him, too. Now after some traumatic life event, of course, many people will go through the experience of getting furious with God. That may just be a phase of the process of healing, so I am not criticizing you if you are, or have, gone through that experience. We just want to pass through that anger and not make it our new home.

When I talk to people about gratitude, this question comes up in many guises: "I understand that the Bible says to give thanks for everything in my life—but you don't expect me to give thanks for sin, do you?" Well, no. Here we need to distinguish between fleshly-minded judgment which impedes gratitude, and discernment which aids it. When we try to approach gratitude from our fleshly mind, we want to give thanks for the things that please us, that are light or easy. But we refuse to give thanks for things that are difficult, painful, or heavy.

But when we approach gratitude from a point of discernment, we thank God for things that are pleasing to Him, for the manifestations of His providence even before we necessarily understand them. But we hate the things that are hateful to Him, even if they are pleasant to us. And so we hate sin; it is not a gift from God. When tempted, we pray for deliverance. When we fall, we pray for forgiveness. But this is still in the context of praising the God who loves human beings and does everything to assist us.

And what, people ask, about times when a person might be forced unwillingly to participate in a sinful activity? Not only praise, but also petition, repentance, and deliverance are the aspects of prayer that our Lord modeled for us in the "Our Father." So in a desperate moment, we stay connected to God through short and urgent prayer—"Help me!" Often that is enough. Afterwards the bully or the abuser bears the sin; we pray to God for healing of the conscience. When *the days are evil* (Eph. 5:16), redeem them through prayer.

Or again, the question takes another form: "Surely you don't expect me to give thanks when I have been sinned against?" It takes great spiritual maturity to do this. People who have mastered this high step of gratitude are motivated by the thought that they are being corrected indirectly, by the hand of God, for hidden sins they may have committed at some time in their life. They believe the saying that God only punishes once, and that chastisement here frees us from punishment in the afterlife. Rather than a narrow, tit-for-tat view of justice, they understand that divine justice has an enormously broad scope. What looks like injustice from the hand of another may, indeed, be justice from the hand of God. If the other person has sinned, God will see to that without our poor attempts to balance the scales in the present moment.

Others who give thanks for being sinned against are motivated by gratitude for all that God has done for them. St. Paisios calls this *filotimo,* or responsive gratefulness (see Ageloglou, 1998, p. 57). If Christ patiently bore the sins against Him, unto death on the Cross, for my sake, should I not show my gratitude by bearing the sins of others for His sake?

A most amazing textbook on how to trust God and offer gratitude in times of tribulation, and even persecution, is the Akathist of Thanksgiving also known as "Glory to God for All

Things." This hymn was written by Metropolitan Tryphon around 1929, shortly before his repose. He was a spiritual father to many and this work, his legacy, has been widely embraced in the Orthodox world. While the injustices and persecutions of the Communist regime were raging unchecked, he chose to focus on God's providence revealed in the beauties of nature, through human arts, in the Church, and in the plan of salvation. He only touches on the trials of life.

Akathist hymns are composed in 13 sections, and he waits until the tenth to say:

> Glory to Thee for every happening, every condition Thy Providence has put me in.
> Glory to Thee for what Thou dost speak to me in my heart.
> Glory to Thee for what Thou dost reveal to me, asleep or awake.
> Glory to Thee for scattering our vain imaginations.
> Glory to Thee for raising us from the slough of our passions through suffering.
> Glory to Thee for curing our pride of heart by humiliation.
> Glory to Thee, O God, from age to age [Ikos 10].

Met. Tryphon, in this hymn, gives us a model. He does not focus on the injustices of the time or the sins of the atheist regime. He follows St. Paul's advice to the Philippians:

> Whatsoever things are true, whatsoever things are honest, whatsoever things are just, whatsoever things are pure, whatsoever things are lovely, whatsoever things are of good report; if there be any virtue, and if there be any praise, think on these things [4:8].

Met. Tryphon focuses on the uplifting things; but when he does mention life's difficulties, it is to look at how divine providence uses even these events for our salvation.

Thus far we have looked at how spiritual joy and gratitude differ from their worldly counterparts, namely, in their being focused on our relationship with God. The various impediments to joy and gratitude have one thing in common: They seek to superimpose a worldly understanding of those virtues onto a spiritual framework. And it doesn't work. This approach means to evaluate or judge a situation, see that we have gained some benefit, and only then to praise God. If there is nothing obviously beneficial then we are stuck—giving lukewarm thanks at best, or else, living in the honesty of our anger, despair, or indifference. Instead, we have seen that spiritual joy and gratitude are based in the sure confidence that God is working things out the best way. And I will add here, that He is working things out delicately, giving scope to the free human will of the billions of people now walking this earth and across the generations from the first to the last. We have seen that gratitude is a creative way in which we can cooperate with divine providence and invite grace into a situation or into our lives.

Gratitude: The Matrix of Community

Giving thanks always for all things unto God, even the Father,
in the name of our Lord Jesus Christ;
Submitting yourselves one to another in the fear of God
(Eph. 5:20, 21).

L ET US BROADEN our sights to include, not only our-selves, God, and His gifts to us, but also how grati-tude informs our relationships with one another. St. Anthony the Great once said: "Our life and our death is with our neighbor. If we gain our brother, we have gained God, but if we scandalize our brother, we have sinned against Christ" (Curley, 2017, p. 47). How does gratitude help us to gain, rather than offend, our brother or sister and thus gain, rather than offend, God? How does it help move us into mutual submission? Let's approach this by looking at examples of a judgmental approach versus a spiritual approach. We'll take examples that come up for couples and families.

In creating these little vignettes, I will be drawing on 30 years of monastic life lived in community and well over a decade of psychotherapy practice. I will be drawing in broad strokes from what I have learned about human nature and interactions over those years. If anything sounds familiar I wish to reassure you that it only means we're all human—you, me, or another person I may have reminded you of—and not that I have based these sketches on anyone in particular. The principles illustrated here in family life can be extrapolated to the larger communities of parishes and monasteries.

Let's start with a couple. They are well matched and enjoy many things in common. But the husband has the habit of dropping his dirty socks on the floor instead of putting them in the hamper. The wife has asked him many times to no avail. Sometimes she vents—"Why can't you just put the socks in the hamper—it's not that hard!" Sometimes she broods. It's worse to ask and be ignored in something so easy than not to speak up at all. Every time she stoops to pick up the socks she feels defeated and angry. And when he wants her to change something, the socks become ammunition— "Well what about you! You never pick up after yourself!"

What can the wife do differently to break the cycle? How can gratitude help? Next time she sees the socks she could say a short prayer of praise or thanksgiving: "Glory to God for all things!" or "Thank you, Lord, for the blessings hidden in this moment." If she can come to a thought of *philotimo*— responsive gratefulness—she might say, "Thank you, Jesus, for being patient with me a thousand times a day. Help me be patient now."

When she is praying for her husband in her morning or evening prayers she can add something longer: "Lord, thank you for the daily reminders that my husband is a complete, free person. Although he loves me, he is not obligated to follow my script for our life together." Or she could say, "Thank you, Lord, for your spiritual image in his heart. Help me to help him manifest that more every day." She can be as creative as she wants—the point is to direct the thoughts to God and His goodness. She'll begin to feel more peaceful toward her husband and be more joyful when she sees him after work. Maybe after some time of working on her own attitude, she'll broach the question again, but it will have a completely different feel. She won't put him in the bind of feeling that if he cooperates he loses—no one likes that. Maybe he'll start picking up the socks and maybe not, but either way, they will have a more harmonious marriage.

Now let's envision the transforming power of gratitude in a family situation with higher stakes than the smelly socks: The family has three children from middle school through high school. The middle-born child, a girl, is head strong and won't listen to parental limits or common sense. She's experimenting with "fire," as they say, and the parents don't want her to end up a "statistic." Something needs to change, and to change soon. The parents are extra stressed and fighting more; the other siblings are resenting all the attention and energy the middle sister is getting.

This is not a situation for gratitude alone. They may need to enlist a family therapist or some other external help. The parents need help in calming their own stress. Their hearts will have to rediscover gratitude toward the daughter in incremental steps. I'm thinking of the "I'm-so-grateful-you're-here" feeling they had when she was first born. But for now, they can start with slow, deep breathing coupled with remembering what it is to feel grateful for something, anything. They can start with five minutes at a time whenever they can work it in. Before bed is a good time, so that peaceful thoughts can give them a restorative night's sleep.

Then they can move toward remembering what it feels like to be grateful for one another. At this stage of the game, most of their interactions have been focused on troubleshooting and problem solving. Despite the issues at home, they need some time to themselves. They need to look each other deeply in the eyes, hold hands, and remember why they are together. Although it will feel delightful when they enter that "zone," as they say, it will be difficult and one or both spouses will resist it. Their hearts have been on the defensive for so long, they are afraid to let down the guard. Old habits of blaming one another when they are disappointed in life will die hard.

The good news is they don't both have to discover their grateful feelings at the same time. Let the husband or the wife resolve to make a long list of the things they were grateful for in the other when they first met, as well as over the years. Add to that the spiritual attributes—"You were made in the image of God. He loves you and wants you near Him for eternity." Then resolve to greet the other in the morning with a heart made sunny by these reflections. Stress is contagious, but so is gratitude. A day begun this way will be a good day. As the parents learn to de-stress and find refreshment in gratitude toward God and one another, divine providence will more easily assist them in the family problems. They will remember, and find ways, to give more attention to the other children.

Perhaps by now they will be pleasantly surprised to find that their "problem child" calms down some as parental unity is restored. In some cases, a child's acting out is like a pressure valve for marital stress; when the stress calms down, so does the child. But if not, the parents will learn to take pressure off themselves to project a perfect appearance to the outside world. Their job is not to have a perfect-looking family or force the child to make good choices, but to assist in the education of her free will. As a wise abbess once said, we pray that our loved ones will be saved "before the end," not right now. We do not know what experiences the good God plans to lead them through so that they can grow in love and wisdom. If we are praying for them to be saved right now, that is more about our comfort than their salvation.

What can we distill from those two vignettes? First, there's a part of our fleshly mind that tracks whether or not we're being taken advantage of in social situations. It can be very helpful in business and market contexts, but we have to tame it down if we want to function optimally in family settings where cooperation rather than competition should be the operating model. Gratitude toward our family can help us love them and, when needed, hold them accountable in a way they can agree to, without feeling they've just been defeated.

And, second, in the case of deep-seated family problems or heart-wrenching tragedies, we may have to approach gratitude incrementally. Remembering to be grateful has to be coupled with learning to manage the stress. Thanksgiving to God does not ignore real problems—there's no flight from reality here—but we thank God for the blessings hidden in the present dire situation. *Faith is the substance of things hoped for* (Heb. 11:1). Expressing gratitude for blessings not yet manifest is a direct and practical expression of faith.

Radical gratitude

I HAVE FOCUSED on family examples thus far because first we need to practice gratitude with those whom we know and love before we aspire to the greater virtue of feeling grateful for those who may be very different from us in culture and background, or even values and agendas. It is harder to express gratitude for people concerning whom we may struggle for basic empathy, who may feel like, or actually be, enemies. So here I entrust you to the words of a prayer by St. Nikolai Velimirović in *Prayers by the Lake*.

> Bless my enemies, O Lord. Even I bless them and do not curse them.
>
> Enemies have driven me into Thine embrace more than friends have. Friends have bound me to earth; enemies have loosed me from earth and have demolished all my aspirations in the world. ...
>
> Truly, enemies have cut me loose from the world and have stretched out my hands to the hem of Thy garment. ...
>
> Bless them and multiply them; multiply them and make them even more bitterly against me—

so that my fleeing to You may have no return;

so that absolute serenity may begin to reign in my soul;

so that my heart may become the grave of my two evil twins: arrogance and anger;

so that I might amass all my treasure in heaven ... .

One hates his enemies only when he fails to realize that they are not his enemies, but cruel friends.

It is truly difficult for me to say who has done me more good and who has done me more evil in the world: friends or enemies.

Therefore bless, O Lord, both my friends and my enemies [c. 1989 pp. 142–144].

In conclusion

WE CAN FOSTER HABITS of gratitude in our lives by remembering the gratitude triangle: God, us, and God's blessings toward us. Some life situations are, indeed, tragic, and some unfold against our wills. Giving thanks authentically is not about judging a bad situation to be good and then giving thanks. Nor is it a hunt for some tiny little speck that pleases us while we judge the whole situation to be bad. Rather, it is about abandoning judgement for discernment. We give thanks for God's providential assistance and for everything that is according to His will. Like Vladika Tryphon, from amidst the storms of life we can still give thanks for past blessings, for the beauties and drama of nature, for human creativity, and for the economy of our salvation. We can turn our minds and hearts to *whatsoever things are true ... whatsoever things are lovely* and be refreshed by those reflections. Like St. Nikolai we can give thanks and bless those who oppress us, who seek to destroy what we have built up, who leave us needy and ashamed. And we can also imitate Christ who praised the Father in the midst of scarcity thus working miracles. When we give thanks for the hidden blessings in a dire situation, we open the door for divine providence to miraculously transform it for us.

Giving thanks for the people in our lives is part of that larger framework of giving thanks in the midst of every life situation. We learn to do this in intimate relationships, so that it can translate to our wider circles, and to society and nation. Our gratitude helps those around us to feel wanted and appreciated. When we lack appreciation for our neighbor, what attitudes fill the void? Resentment and all of its accomplices: indifference, self-centeredness, contempt, envy, and even fear. When people feel those negative attitudes from us, they are likely to react with defensiveness. Then disagreements follow in which it's never really clear what we are fighting about, because it's not about the words. It's about the tone of voice ... the glaring eyes ... the aggressive posture. In short, it's about the attitude.

On the other hand, gratitude clears the path toward mutual respect; when we maintain a grateful attitude toward our brother or sister in Christ, our positive attitude invites reciprocation. *Philotimo* motivates us to a healthy competition to be kind to one another. Then we have gained our brother or sister for Christ's sake and it becomes easier to have mutual submission, which is the external manifestation of our mutual respect. Then our marriages, families, and communities will live as a reflection of the harmonious life of the Holy Trinity, although with temptations and trials in this present world. And, through grateful participation in these relationships, we hope to be made worthy of the unfading Kingdom. Amen.

REFERENCES AND BIBLIOGRAPHY
THIRD ESSAY

Ageloglou, (Priestmonk) Christodoulos. (1998). *Elder Paisios of the Holy Mountain.* Holy Mountain.

Beck, Schaeffer & Kriegel, P. C., (Trans.). (1993). *The explanation by Blessed Theophylact, Archbishop of Ochrid and Bulgaria, of the Holy Gospel according to St. Mark.* House Springs, MO: Chrysostom.

Chitty, Derwas J., (Trans.). (1975/1991). *The letters of Saint Antony the Great.* Fairacres, Oxford: SLG.

Curley, (Archabbot) Anthony. (2017). *Sayings of the Desert Fathers: The thirty eight sayings of St. Anthony the Great.* Nashua, MT: Monastery of Mary in the Wilderness.

Hammarskjöld, Dag. (1959/2006). *Markings,* (L. Sjoberg, Trans.). New York, NY: Vintage.

Martin, James. (2011). *Between heaven and mirth: Why joy, humor, and laughter are at the heart of the spiritual life.* New York, NY: Harper One.

_____. (2018). "Between heaven and mirth" in *The Science of Laughter.* New York, NY: Time.

Roccas, Nicole M. (2017). *Time and despondency: Regaining the present in faith and life.* Chesterton, IN: Ancient Faith.

Saliers, Don. (1980/2011). *The soul in paraphrase: Prayer and the religious affections.* White Sulphur Springs, WV: The Order of St. Luke.

Smith, R. Payne, (Trans.). (1983). *Commentary on the Gospel of Saint Luke by Saint Cyril, Patriarch of Alexandria.* Astorion, OR: Studion.

Ten Boom, Cornelia with Sherrill, J. & Sherrill, C. (1971). *The hiding place.* Old Tappan, NJ: Spire Books.

Trenchard, Warren C. (1998). *Complete vocabulary guide to the Greek New Testament.* Revised ed. Grand Rapids, MI: Zondervan.

Velimirović, (Bishop) Nikolai. (1922/c. 1989). *Prayers by the lake,* (T. Mika, [Archimandrite] and S. Scott, [Priest], Trans.), *A treasury of Serbian Orthodox spirituality,* vol. V. Grayslake, IL: Free Serbian Orthodox Diocese of the USA & Canada.

Printed in Great Britain
by Amazon

23074029R00056